WITH HEART**S**
ON FIRE

WITH HEARTS ON FIRE

THE STORY OF ROBERT & IVY MILLIKEN

❖

*This shall be written for the generation to come:
and the people which shall be created shall
praise the LORD.*

Psalm 102 : 18

AMBASSADOR

BELFAST ◆ **GREENVILLE**
NORTHERN IRELAND · SOUTH CAROLINA

With Hearts On Fire

© Copyright 1997 Robert & Ivy Milliken

ISBN 1 84030 012 4

AMBASSADOR PRODUCTIONS LTD,
Providence House
16 Hillview Avenue,
Belfast, BT5 6JR
Northern Ireland

Emerald House,
1 Chick Springs Road, Suite 206
Greenville,
South Carolina 29609
United States of America

Contents

❖

Forward   Helen Roseveare 7

Chapter 1   An Irish Boy 11

Chapter 2   North Belfast to South Norwood 17

Chapter 3   A Welsh Girl 25

Chapter 4   A New Life 31

Chapter 5   Revival at Imbai's 37

Chapter 6   Wedding Drums 45

Chapter 7   First-Fruits 51

Chapter 8   Going Home 61

Chapter 9   First Furlough 69

Chapter 10   Consolidation 77

Chapter 11   Revival Reaches Malingwia 85

Chapter 12   Second Furlough 95

Chapter 13   Unexpected Exit 103

Chapter 14   Another Door Opens 109

Chapter 15   Generation to Generation 115

Chapter 16   Back to Courrières 121

Chapter 17   Aylsham Finale 127

Chapter 18   A Home in Hampshire 135

Postscript   141

Foreword

❖

I FIRST MET BOBBY AND IVY MILLIKEN AT IBAMBI AT OUR TRIENNIAL MISSIONARIES' CONFERENCE, EARLY IN 1954. I had been in the Belgian Congo less than a year, and they were already veterans of twenty years missionary experience - but together we had witnessed great things that past year. That year had seen wonderful events in the WEC area of responsibility, in the north-eastern province of this vast equatorial country. God had chosen, in answer to the persistent believing prayers of many of His children, African and European, to pour out His Holy Spirit upon the waiting Church. Revival had swept through the region, from the far south at Mulito and Lubutu, through the midland areas of Ibambi and Wamba, and on up to Poko and Malingwia in the far north-west.

As we gathered in Conference, there was a great expectancy that the Lord would yet do even greater things amongst the missionaries. Jack Scholes led the Bible Studies, teaching from the first 8 chapters of Leviticus - how we can approach our Holy Lord God only through humble sacrifice, linked to Romans 12:1,2: "Present yourselves as living sacrifices .." - and indeed, one after another sought to do just that. Then we had testimonies from each of the stations as to the work of the Holy Spirit in all the outlying churches. And I will never forget Ivy's radiant face as she told us of the outpouring at Malingwia, the changed lives, the new church in fact.

I sat beside her, at the long trestle table in the Bible School hall, for the midday meal, just to listen .. and listen .. as she spoke of all that had occurred years before at Imbais, and now again at Malingwia. She was just so totally in love with her Lord, that as she spoke, I did not see or hear her, but rather HIM of whom she spoke. Now today, as I have read through her life-story, partly told by herself, partly by her devoted husband Bobby, I have revelled in living through those wonderful days again.

Yes, when I had the privilege of re-visiting Zaire in 1989, sixteen years after leaving to come home to serve as an itinerant deputation worker, I went to Malingwia for thirty-six hours. I shared with a packed church, some thoughts on Relationships - firstly, the basis between each one of us and God, being yoked to Him; secondly, as an outflow of the first, our resultant relationship with one another, in service, 'washing one another's feet' as Jesus commanded us and my interpreter broke down and wept. Immediately, there was a great surge of the Holy Spirit throughout the Church, and over thirty young men came forward, without any appeal or specific call, and pled with God for cleansing. Someone stood and reminded the older folk of the ministry of the Millikens in their midst thirty years before - and again a great surge of godly power, and another crowd of older men and women swept forward, weeping and pleading with God for cleansing. The foundation work laid all those years ago is still bearing fruit - to God be all the glory!

More recently, when itinerating in South England, and speaking at their son, Robert's church in Portsmouth, once again I sat beside these saints of God. Oh, yes, they had aged: they were not quite so physically active: they had been through the fires in Zaire, in France and in Great Britain. But they were still both radiant, deeply in love with their Saviour, and with no greater joy in their lives than to lead another to His feet. They were so totally self-effacing, uninterested in talking about themselves, always interested in others and listening to whatever they might have to share .. and so quickly and simply, without any apparent effort, guiding the conversation round, so that they could speak of the One they loved beyond all others. What a privilege to be asked to write a short foreword to their life story!

As you read the following pages, keep looking up into the face of the One they seek to glorify, and realise that He can do through you exactly what He has done through them, if you are equally willing to hand over everything - yes, everything - whatever the cost may appear to be. Entrust your dearest to Him, who can keep it safe unto that glorious Coming Day. Launch out into the deep and let the Master make YOU into a 'fisher of men'. Nothing would have brought greater joy to Ivy and Bobby than that this simply-told story of the lives of two devoted servants of God should stir someone else to give their all to Him, and see what He can do with a "lump of ordinary clay."

"Have Thine own way, Lord,
Have Thine own way:
Thou art the Potter,
I am the clay.
Mould me and make me
After Thy will,
While I am waiting
Yielded and still"

A.A.Pollard, 1862-1934.

That was certainly the prayer in the hearts of both of these veterans, as they set out on their pilgrimage: and as we pray the same prayer, may we watch God work the same transformation in each of our lives.

Helen Roseveare
August 1995.

Chapter One

An Irish Boy

❖

MY SUNDAY SCHOOL ATTENDANCE CARD WAS STAMPED
WITH A SHAMROCK STAMP EVERY SUNDAY MORNING -
so I knew I was Irish! We lived in North Belfast in the Ardoyne, not
far trom the Shankhill Road, and went to Sunday school at the
Woodvale Presbyterian Church - and not only to Sunday school.
My Mother was a devout Christian. She sent the six of us - the five
girls and me - to the ten o'clock Sunday school and then on to the
eleven o'clock morning service while she cooked Sunday dinner.
Then it was Sunday school again in the afternoon. Mother came
with us to the evening service and we completely filled the 'Milliken
pew'. All the services were packed. Opposite was the 'Miller pew'
where my Mother's eldest sister, Aunt Annie, sat with her family.

Aunt Annie lived across the road and she ran one of Grandfather
Ferguson's butcher's shops, which meant that my Mother looked
after her children much of the time - we all grew up together. Grandfather Ferguson had a cattle farm out at Castlereagh. I loved going
out to his farm during the school holidays and later when I grew
older I would help in the butcher's shop on Saturdays earning pocket
money working the sausage-making machine.

Father did not come with us to Church, except on family occasions, but he did nothing to hinder or discourage us. Like his Father, he was an engineer - a chargehand in the shipyard. Grandfather Milliken was an engineer in a large spinning mill - the largest in the world at that time. So I suppose it isn't surprising that I was trained in engineering too. Both Grandfathers were a great help to us - especially when my Father was away at the War. That's one of my earliest memories: I was their third child, born in October 1908, and when I was nearly six I remember my Father announcing to us that he was going away to be a soldier because the army needed engineers. "Will you have a soldier's belt?" I asked. It was August 1914 when he joined the Royal Engineers and shortly afterwards was sent to France. After he left us Mother turned to me and said, "You're the only man in the house now, Robert".

Once a year Father came home on leave - he always took us out for a ride in the country in a hired pony and trap. His brother - my Uncle Bob - also joined up. He went into the navy as an engineer. His ship was torpedoed and, though he was rescued from the sea, he never really recovered and died young. Grandfather Milliken was an elder in the Presbyterian Church and years later, when I told him that I was going to be a missionary, he told me that Uncle Bob had wanted to be a missionary and that I was "fulfilling his commission".

I went to the local Fresbyterian school; I remember it was in two sections, girls upstairs, boys downstairs. Mr. McKeckney was Headmaster of the Boy's School. He taught music and was also choirmaster at the Church connected with the school. One of the songs he taught us began "Away, away at break of day". Twenty years or so later, I was playing the tune on my mouth organ as we sat on the verandah of our mission bungalow deep in the Congo. My wife said "That tune could be used for a hymn in Bangala", then she composed a hymn about the life and work of Jesus - it came so easily and quickly. When we were on our first furlough I went to see Mr. McKeckney and told him how that Bangala hymn came to be written. Mr. McKeckney was overjoyed; he said, "This week I am retiring from school teaching and this is God's benediction upon my work here".

Every Sunday afternoon before we went to Sunday school we would receive a visit from an elderly white-haired man named Mr.Boyd. He had worked in the shipyard and had nearly lost his job because he was such a hopeless drunkard, but Father helped him to keep it. Then he had been converted. So every week he came to pray with the family. He came to pray for God's blessing on us and for Father's safe return - and he did come home safely about a year after the war ended.

In 1920 the evangelist W.P. Nicholson came to Belfast. Thousands were influenced by his powerful preaching - hundreds made professions of conversion. Men at the shipyards went straight from their work to the meetings without going home. Dad's sisters went to the meetings - but not Dad! Some of my Sisters made decisions for Christ - but not me! They would come home singing:

"Dare to be a Daniel - Dare to stand alone
Dare to pass the public house - And take
your money home".

By this time I was nearly thirteen and had joined the Boy's Brigade. Mr. Coulter the B.B. Captain, was a very godly man and faithfully taught us the Gospel. Here I was, then, with a background of regular church-going, surrounded by godly influences and in the midst of evangelical fervour, and yet completely resistant to it all.

At school I loved playing football and when I was sixteen my friends began to laugh at me for continuing to go to Sunday School. They said I was too old for Sunday School and should be out playing football with them. When I told my Mother she gave me this advice: "Never be ashamed of the Lord Jesus, Robert, because He was not ashamed to die on the cross for you". I've never forgotten her words.

Then the time came to leave school. My Father wanted me to become an engineer like his Father and Brother. He took me round the shipyard to see what the work was like. Then he sent me along to my Grandfather's mill - and it was there that I was taken on as an apprentice mechanical engineer, that was in 1924.

During the War my Mother had taken to keeping pigs in an old stable yard at the back of our house - and later on goats as well. She was a true farmer's daughter and a shrewd business woman. Several of my school friends used to earn their pocket money by cleaning out the stables for her. One of them was Tom Telford. Mother was very fond of him and he was always hanging around our house. One day I remarked that Tom was a real Christian. "That's what you should be", she replied.

I was a year into my apprenticeship and just turned seventeen when my dear Mother suddenly took ill and died. It was Christmas 1925. Mother was busy caring for the family and, not wanting to spoil our celebrations, said nothing about the pain in her side. By the time Christmas was over and she had been admitted to hospital appendicitis had turned to peritonitis. There was no penicillin in those days. She never recovered from the operation. It was a terrible shock.

My oldest sister, Lily, took over the home but things were never the same. The animals went, and Dad let a man with a taxi keep his vehicle in part of the stables. I used to try and drive it when no one was around - and I liked to watch Dad tuning and stripping down car engines. That stood me in good stead years later out in the Congo.

As the years passed my Sisters married and left home until only the two youngest were left living with Dad. Eventually they too wanted to leave, so my Father moved in with one of my married Sisters and the family home was sold. That was during the second World War. Father had only been out of the old house a few months when a bomb fell in our street and completely demolished it. The couple who had just moved in were both killed.

However, to return to 1926: by then I had joined a football team. One snowy Thursday (it was the 4th March - less than three months after my Mother had passed away) we went to the ground to practice but the snow was too deep and we had to go home. On the way I met Tom Telford.

"Will you come to the meeting tonight?" he asked. I didn't want to go and began to mumble and make excuses about having too much homework, but he would have none of it. Of course, with my background I had a fair idea what these meetings were all about. "Will they button-hole me?" I asked. "I'm just as good as any Christian. I don't smoke or drink, I go to church every week ...." "You can't be saved by your good works", Tom replied.

Tom was right and I knew it but I wasn't yet willing to yield my life to the Lord. Nevertheless Tom persisted and I went with him to our church's little mission hall in Disraeli Street just off the Shankhill Road. After the meeting had finished Tom turned to me and said, "Won't you give your heart to the Lord, Robert?" I knew that I had been resisting the Holy Spirit and was disobedient to God. There and then I made up my mind. "I will!", I said. Tom was so amazed he nearly fell off his chair. Then he called an elderly man over. He talked with me and asked me to pray with him. Those precious moments remain so vivid in my memory. Perspiration broke out all over me as he prayed - I was making a real decision, there was no going back now. Then he asked me to pray. All that came stumbling out was a sentence of grateful praise,

"Thank you Lord that you have saved me tonight" - and, praise His name, He had! The chains had fallen off. I was a new man in Christ. What relief! What joy!

Tom then opened his Bible and turned to Romans chapter 10; he read verse 9 to me: "That if thou shalt confess with thy mouth the Lord Jesus, and shalt believe in thine heart that God hath raised Him from the dead, thou shalt be saved."

"Now go home and tell someone you've been saved", he counselled.

With a joyful heart and a light step I made my way home. There was my sister Lily; she had made a decision for Christ at one of W.P. Nicholson's meetings so I told her what had happened earlier that evening. Before I went to bed I found my Bible and started to read it. I had read parts of the Bible before - as a duty, a task to fulfil for Bible class, a verse to learn as a Sunday school assignment - but now I was reading it voluntarily. Thus I opened my Bible and began to read from the beginning, and as I read the Book of Genesis it seemed so fresh - as if it was a completely new Book to me. My spiritual eyes were opening - the Bible had become the Word of God.

So ended a remarkable day - Thursday 4th March 1926 - a never-to-be-forgotten day of days. The Lord Jesus Christ had become my own Saviour and Lord. My outlook was completely changed, my life never the same again.

•••

"Therefore if any man be in Christ, he is a new creature: old things are passed away; behold, all things are become new."

II Corinthians 5 : 17

Chapter Two

North Belfast to South Norwood

❖

THE NEXT MORNING WHILE AT WORK IN THE MILL I TOLD ONE OF MY WORKMATES THAT I HAD BECOME A Christian. His reaction surprised me: "Don't be a hypocrite. Be a real one", he immediately responded. Later I met my former Sunday School teacher and told her. I was even more surprised by her reply - "I've just become one myself", she said!

That evening Tom took me along to a lady's house where they were holding a farewell meeting for two young men who were leaving Belfast to join the Missionary Training Colony in London - Jim Grainger and Sam Elder.

Jim Grainger went to the Congo the following year and Sam Elder in 1929. Sam had been a U.V.F. gun man during 'the troubles' and was converted while serving his sentence in Crumlin Road jail. They spoke about their call to Africa to serve with the Heart of Africa Mission (as the Worldwide Evangelisation Crusade was then known). That was the first I heard of either the Missionary Training Colony or W.E.C. - the day after my conversion. As we were leaving the lady of the house said to me "Perhaps one day we'll be sending you out too".

Straight after the missionary meeting an open-air witness had been arranged. We all stood in a ring and sang hymns accompanied by Tom on his accordion. Tom was as bold as I was embarrassed - especially when some of my footballing friends came along and started jeering - but Tom thrust me forward urging me to tell them what had happened the previous evening. So for the first time I 'gave my testimony' - and very nervous I was too! The real crunch, however, came the following morning. Saturday morning was always reserved for football training but the crowd I was now with went 'tracting'. So was it to be football training or tract distribution? My brief football career ended abruptly - I knew I had to be different.

While we were out tracting somewhere along the Antrim coast I got talking with Bob Snoddon. He had been a real Christian for years and a great friend of Jim Grainger. He realised that I needed fellowship with other young Christians if I was to maintain spiritual momentum and so he said, "Will you be my pal now that Jim's gone to London? You come along with me". So Bob became my friend and I went with him to the Methodist Church. Tom Telford continued at the Presbyterian Church and gradually dropped out of my life. Looking back I can see God's hand in my transfer to the Methodist Church, they had a sound pastor and a large and keen group of young people, exactly what a young convert needed to keep him on the straight and narrow way. Years later, during our first furlough, I met up with Tom Telford again. He came round to the W.E.C. regional headquarters in Belfast where we were staying, but all he could talk about was politics. He had been so courageous and keen for the Lord, he had been instrumental in my coming to Christ and now, twenty years on, all he could talk about was politics. How very sad! Eventually Tom admitted that he too had been challenged at a missionary meeting to volunteer for service in West Africa with the Qua Iboe Mission, but he had resisted the call. Later he married a girl belonging to the Salvation Army, settled down and became involved in social work. From that it was but a short step into politics.

Now that I was a Christian every evening was taken up with some activity. On Monday I continued with evening classes at the technical college, Tuesday was Christian Endeavour at the Methodist Church, Wednesday I was back at the technical college night school, Thursday was the missionary prayer meeting at The Welcome Mission, Friday the open-air witness, and Saturdays tracting and special church meetings.

It was that missionary prayer meeting at "The Welcome" each Thursday which gave me my missionary vision. It was known as "the prayer battery" and was chiefly concerned with the needs facing W.E.C. missionaries. The Welcome Mission had been founded by Amy Wilson Carmichael as an outreach to Belfast mill girls before she went to India. From the outset it had a strong interest in overseas mission and a good number of men and women were sent to the mission field from "The Welcome".

One night at the prayer battery it was announced that Mrs. C.T. Studd was coming to Belfast and that she was to speak at a special meeting in the YMCA Hall. We eagerly awaited that Saturday and when it came a party of young people from the Methodist Church went along to the YMCA. The hall was packed to capacity. Mrs. Studd was accompanied by some missionaries on furlough from the Congo. They showed slides and spoke of the work and sang songs in Bangala. Little did I realise that just a few years later I would be singing the same songs in the same language. Then Mrs. Studd got up to give the message. She was a dynamic, aristocratic Irish Lady and the atmosphere became electric. She told of her husband's call to the Congo at the age of fifty-three, of his desire to win the Congo basin for Christ as a bulwark against the advance if Islam into southern Africa, of the great opportunities and the great need. She said how, though elderly and ill, he had returned to central Africa and was still out there serving the Lord Jesus. Then she turned to us young people and said "You can be a Christian and live as you like - but the day will come when you have to give an account of how you have spent your life. 'Only one life t'will soon be past, only what's done for Christ will last'." Then she repeated her husband's stirring motto:

"If Jesus Christ be God and died for me
then no sacrifice can be too great for me to make for Him".

There in the YMCA Hall I responded to that call as I said in my heart, "Yes Lord, I am willing to be a missionary".

Of course, I was still only eighteen. When I got home I told my Father about it and added, "Do you remember how Uncle Bob always wanted to be a missionary?". Father's response was "Well, that doesn't mean you have to be one". Then he advised me to complete my apprenticeship before I made any move. I think he thought that the notion would pass with the passing of the years, but that desire to serve overseas never left me. Grandfather Milliken's reaction was different; he said that I would be "fulfilling Uncle Bob's commission".

Later I wrote to W.E.C. in London about my call to the mission field and their advice was the same as Father's - finish your apprenticeship first. And so the round of Sunday worship, daily work, evening meetings, and Saturday rallies and outreach continued with one major addition to the schedule. Friday I went along with the Methodist young people to special evening classes at the Belfast Methodist Theological College. There we studied Old Testament history and literature. One of the tutors offered to teach me New Testament Greek but regretfully I declined his offer - my days and nights were filled to capacity.

In 1930 - my apprenticeship successfully completed - I applied to join the Missionary Training Colony in South Norwood, London and was accepted to the session commencing in March the following year. The Missionary Training Colony had been started in 1919 by C.T. Studd's sons-in-law, Alfred Buxton and Gilbert Barclay. By the time I arrived, Alfred's brother, Godfrey Buxton, was leading the work. Alfred Buxton had accompanied C.T. Studd on his pioneering reconnaissance expedition to North East Congo in 1913. After a disagreement with C.T. Studd over mission policy he returned to Britain in 1927 and gathered recruits for a new mission to central Africa. He had left the Missionary Training Colony in the charge of his brother, Captain Godfrey Buxton, when he returned to Africa in 1920. The Colony was located in a series of ex-army nissen huts and run on military lines like a pioneer camp with Captain Buxton as its "Commandant". There were about thirty trainees. The MTC did not charge any fees - in fact it gave its students pocket money - but as a sign of God's leading, each new student had to bring an unsolicited gift of £10. In Belfast the weeks had dwindled to days and still the money hadn't come in. By the day of departure, I was getting really worried but I didn't mention it to anybody. As I was getting on the ferry, Dad slipped me a £10 note. Little did he realise the significance of that gift.

Every month we chose a new 'President' whose duty was to wake everyone up and a new cook to help Mrs. Buxton with the meals. The training given was essentially practical, designed to make candidates self-disciplined, equipped to face the most primitive conditions. Every morning we were awakened at 6 a.m. for physical training (P.T.) and running. This was followed by a "Russian bath" - you rushed-in and you rushed-out - because it was freezing cold. Personal 'quiet-time' was from 7.00 until 8.00, then it was breakfast - porridge with syrup, milk and bread. The rest of the morning was spent in Bible study. We went through the books of the Bible systematically and each of us had to write an essay on each book studied - my first one was on Ezekiel. What an assignment! However, to my surprise Mr. Buxton said it was the best among that set of essays - but I had to give the credit where it belonged - to those five years of evening classes in Old Testament with the Methodists back in Belfast. Our afternoons were spent in language study according to the field in which we hoped to serve.

There were also lectures in tropical medicine and we all did a spell of practical work down at Croydon Hospital mostly in the casualty department. The team that I was with included one of 'the three Freds' - one of them came from Belfast, and all three were martyred by Amazonian Indians while serving with the Unevangelised Fields Mission in Colombia. The nurses in the casualty department used to let me stitch up wounds because they reckoned that I was the neatest stitcher. Once a man was brought into casualty whose scalp had been almost torn off in an accident involving a lift. The doctor told me to start stitching one side while he did the other and we met in the middle - the man was under anaesthetic! He recovered!

Every Friday we went to the dentist who taught us how to extract teeth. This proved very useful when I was out in the Congo. It enabled me to relieve the suffering of dozens of Africans out in the villages, which in turn led to an opportunity to share the Gospel with them.

The months of July and August were given over to evangelistic trekking. My first trek was down in Cornwall. The team's only means of transport was one bike. A scout was sent ahead on the bike to make contact with a church and offer our services. The rest of us had to walk pushing our trek cart. After two months our feet were very sore. We had a tent to sleep in and local Christians gave us food. During the trek we had a week known as "2 by 2" when we had to learn how to live 'by faith'. We were each given half-a-crown (12p) and sent out in pairs to evangelise a locality. During my week away from the team there was only one night when we slept out under a haystack. Next morning the farmer's wife saw us and said, "What are you doing there? Why didn't you tell us you needed a bed for the night?" She gave us breakfast. We came back with our half crowns! It was when we were on trek that we heard the news that C.T. Studd had passed into glory on July 16th at Ibambi - his last words were "Hallelujah!"

The Missionary Training Colony was within walking distance of W.E.C. Headquarters. I agreed with the spirit and approach of C.T. Studd so I went along to the W.E.C. prayer meetings, which were led by Mr.Norman Grubb and his wife (who was C.T. Studd's younger daughter).

The first half of the two-year course ended in December 1931. I went home for two months along with the rest of the Belfast contingent. Some of us kept up our 'Russian baths' and P.T. right through January and February. I got a job in a Ford motor garage - so became familiar with petrol engines and motor mechanics, and I learned how to drive. Later, before I left for the Congo, Dad gave me a set of car tools. All of this turned out to be crucial preparation for missionary service, just as important as my time at the Training Colony. Most evenings I was engaged in Christian work leading missionary meetings at The Welcome Mission, at The Mustard Seed Mission, and other places.

In March 1932 we returned to the Training Colony for the second half of the course which was organised along the same lines as our first year. My training was completed that December and then I went back to Belfast. From there I wrote to W.E.C. making formal application to serve on the mission field. Mr. Grubb wrote back inviting me to join the next candidates' course starting in January.

So, shortly after the start of the New Year (1933), I returned to London and again made my way to South Norwood - but this time to No. 19 Highland Road. I rang the bell. The door was opened by a young woman who spoke with a Welsh accent:

"I'm Robert Milliken from Belfast," I said, "I've come to join the candidates' course."

"Mrs. Grubb is expecting you", she replied. "She told me to take you straight to her".

"I'm Ivy Roberts - Come, follow me" -

And I have been following her ever since!

•••

*"The Holy Spirit said, 'Now separate to Me Barnabas and
Saul for the work to which I have called them."*
Acts 13 : 2

The first brick house Bobby built in the Congo.

The home Bobby and Ivy lived in at Villenenue in France.

Chapter Three

A Welsh Girl

❖

YOU HAVE READ IN THE FIRST CHAPTER THAT BOBBY WAS BORN IN BELFAST IN OCTOBER 1908. WELL, I WAS born the following month at Gwystre Farm in Radnorshire in mid-Wales. I'm so glad that he was born first! Gwystre Farm is two miles from the hamlet of Gwystre and about five miles from the small town of Llandrindod Wells. There were fourteen children in our family - seven girls and seven boys - the perfect number - I was Number 6! My Mother also came from a large family. They were successful farmers in mid-Wales and all of them born-again Christians. My Father did not have a farming background. He came from a Radnorshire family of boot and shoe makers and lived in Newbridge-on-Wye, not far away, and because he was over six feet tall he became a policeman. Father's family were all converted during the Welsh Revival of 1904. One day, as Father was reading the Bible, the light suddenly shone in his heart and he was born again. When he began walking-out with Mother and asked her to marry him she replied:

"I can't marry a policeman. If you want to marry me you will have to be a farmer".

"All right then, I will," he said, "I'll be a farmer".

And a very good farmer he became too! God blessed him. His first farm was all livestock but by the time I was born we had moved to Gwystre which was a mixed farm.

As the family grew so it became necessary to extend the farmhouse and I can remember Mother saying, "The parlour is your room, Father. You sit and read in here". He was, you see, a lay preacher. He rode to the chapels on horseback. We attended Gwystre Chapel twice every Sunday, which was two miles distant and up a very steep hill. It was too far to go on Sunday afternoon for Sunday school so Father conducted his own Sunday school in our parlour at home. We also held family prayers in the parlour. Father was always reading the Bible - I never saw him read any other book. We took the local weekly newspaper - but he barely glanced at it - yet he knew his Bible so well that he never needed to use a concordance. He was also a gifted musician - he played the violin and was an expert in the Tonic sol-fa method. He taught it to all of us and I learned to play the piano as well. Years later this proved very useful out in the Congo. The Africans picked up Tonic sol-fa so very easily. Round the village fires of an evening I taught them part-singing accompanying them on a concertina. The Africans are as musical as the Welsh!

We held Father in awe. He was very strict; he had to be with fourteen of us! There was just a year between each of us three middle girls - myself, May and Iris - so we were always together. I remember that when we heard Father clattering into the farmyard - he wore farm clogs - we always ran to Mother and asked her to give us some job to do. Otherwise it would be:

"Are these girls helping you Mother? If not I can give them work to do". That meant going out into the fields stone-picking which was a hard back-breaking task. Of course all the boys were automatically expected to be out and about the farm helping him.

Now I will give you a list of the names of my brothers and sisters in order. All the girls were given flower names:

1. Daisy was the eldest - she went to Grammar School and became a teacher and then married and settled in Leominster.

2. Lily was next - she also went to Grammar School and became a teacher, then she went to Redcliffe Bible College and became a missionary in the Congo

3. Hugh - he became a farmer and distributed tracts whenever he went to market.

4. John - went to The Missionary Training Colony and became a missionary in the Congo

5. Scott - he went to Swansea Bible College but he injured his leg on the farm and couldn't go out to the mission field. So he worked in insurance and served as a lay-preacher in Herefordshire.

6. Ivy - that's me.

7. May - she trained as a nurse and became a midwife. She too went to Redcliffe Bible College.

8. Iris - She trained at Mount Hermon College but by then our parents were growing older. So she returned to the farm and helped to run Gwystre Chapel. She later married a Pastor of a Pentecostal Church.

9. Olive - she also trained as a nurse and went to live in Canada.

10. Joseph - he became a very successful farmer and helped to bring up our son.

11. Fred - became a farmer, and had two children.

12. Violet - had three sons all of whom became doctors.

13 James - became a farmer in Brecon and also helped raise our son.

14. Richard - he went to Bristol Baptist College and became a Baptist Minister.

Every single one of us became a truly converted, born-again Christian through Father's influence. In my case it wasn't until I was eleven. You see, I was a bit of a baby and very nervous when I had to leave the village school and go to the grammar school five miles away in Llandrindod Wells. So I summoned up courage to speak to Father and told him that I was frightened to go to the new school and needed to become a real Christian so that I could have God's help. He led me to Christ in the parlour. Eventually May and Iris joined me at the grammar school. Father bought each of us beautiful new bicycles and we cycled there every day - five miles each way.

Llandrindod Wells was a spa town, famous for its waters which were thought to cure rheumatism and arthritis. Visitors flocked to the town in the summer and there were several large hotels - 'The Metropole' was built while I was at school there. During the first week in August there was the annual Bible Convention held in a huge marquee with well known visiting speakers. It was called "The Welsh Keswick," many were converted in that tent, and we as a family were always greatly blessed. Even though it was the middle of the hay-making season (the busiest time on our farm), Father always took us to the Convention. To make sure that we got there in good time we went in his milk float!

When I left school in Llandrindod Wells I became a teacher back at our local primary school in Nantmel where I taught the youngest children in a class where the ages ranged from five to seven. I even taught my own younger brothers and sister - Fred, Violet, James and Richard. Every school day I cycled the four miles to Nantmel on the road to Rhayader. I loved teaching the little ones just into school, away from their mothers for the first time, and they responded to me. Yet is was at that time that God called me to serve Him overseas. It was like this:

Mrs. C.T. Studd was a regular speaker at The Welsh Keswick, and my sister Lily and brother John had already responded to the Lord's call received through her stirring ministry to serve Him in the Congo. By this time Lily was training at Redcliffe, John at The Missionary Training Colony and Scott at Swansea Bible College. So it must have been August 1927 when I heard Mrs. Studd tell of the great response to the Gospel in the Congo and first caught the vision of becoming a missionary myself. I listened to the testimonies of the missionaries and even before Mrs. Studd had finished her appeal I was on my feet, the first one up.

It was two years since Bobby had heard Mrs. Studd at the YMCA Hall in Belfast and she died very suddenly the following year (1928). When I told Father and Mother that I too had received a call to the mission field they were with me one hundred per cent. So I went back to teach at Nantmel School after the summer holiday with a longing to be out in Africa serving African people. Often at home I would go out to the barn to pray for the work in Congo and at times would weep and weep. On one such occasion I was given a vision of Africans beckoning me to come to them - and how I did long to be with them! At that time I had never seen an African but when I reached the Congo I saw that they beckoned each other in exactly the same characteristic way I had seen in that vision.

However, the way did not yet open up for me to begin training. The following summer (1928) I obtained a new teaching post in a different school but it was with a restless, heavy heart. One day I went to telephone to make an appointment with the Head Teacher to see round my new school While I was in the telephone kiosk I heard a voice say, "This is only for a short time". It was so distinct and clear that I turned round to see who was behind me!

Well, I taught for another two years at that school and then in September 1930 I went to Redcliffe Bible College at Chiswick in London. The course lasted two years and it would have been more or less the same two years that Bobby was at The Missionary Training Colony. He was in south London while I was in south-west London but neither of us knew of the other's existence.

There were between thirty and thirty-five young lady students at Redcliffe all in training for the overseas mission field. There were no men which, in my opinion, was a good thing - because most of those girls were about to sacrifice all prospect of finding a husband. During my first year Miss Miall was the College Principal but it was her final year before retirement. Miss Miall was a most impressive lady - a real lady - stately and very beautiful - and yet also a deeply spiritual woman of prayer. She had been a missionary in China and she used to tell us how Satan tries to discourage missionaries out on the field. Miss Miall's manner and teaching left a lasting influence upon me. When she retired Miss Nash became Principal. We didn't live in nissen huts but in a large suburban house. Since ours was a college for young ladies there was no P.E., jogging or 'Russian baths' at 6 o'clock in the morning - but we did study the Bible all the way through.

By the time my course at Redcliffe was completed in 1932 my brother John had been out in the Congo with W.E.C. three years and my sister Lily two years. Back home in Wales it never occurred to me to apply to any other society than W.E.C. I was accepted for their candidates' course beginning in January 1933. At No. 19 Highland Road we were each given jobs to do. Two days after I arrived back in London I was on door bell duty. That morning Mrs. Grubb had taken me aside and given me very clear instructions:

"Now this morning, Ivy, we are expecting a young man from Belfast named Robert Milliken - he too is for the Congo. If the bell rings you must leave the lecture immediately and go to the door. Ask him who he is. If it is Mr. Milliken you must bring him straight to me". It did ring and I obeyed her instructions to the letter!

•••

"The lines are fallen unto me in pleasant places; yea,
I have a goodly heritage".
Psalm 16 : 6

Chapter Four

A New Life

❖

THE CANDIDATES' COURSE LASTED TWO MONTHS. DURING THOSE EIGHT WEEKS WE CANDIDATES GOT TO know one another quite well. Mr. and Mrs. Grubb were already acquainted with both Ivy and me - Ivy through her brother and sister, and me through my attendance at the weekly prayer meeting when I was at the MTC. So it was no surprise when we were both accepted officially for service in the Congo when the course ended in March.

During the previous five years Mr. and Mrs. Grubb had been reorganising and rebuilding the Society's home base. C.T. Studd had prophesied that his grave stone would become a stepping stone. "When I am gone, the Mission will leap ahead", he wrote - and so it did. In 1931 The Heart of Africa Mission had been reduced to thirty-five workers. During the next ten years it grew to over 300 in fourteen different fields. In faith Mr. and Mrs. Grubb had called for ten recruits to volunteer for missionary service in the Congo as a memorial to C.T. Studd by the anniversary of his "glorification". By July 1932 all the necessary equipment and finance had been supplied and ten candidates had come forward.

Rees Howells of Swansea was intimately involved in this advance and, encouraged by his prayer support, Mr. and Mrs. Grubb dared to ask for fifteen new recruits for 1933. C.T. Studd had a burden for all the unevangelised regions of the world; from its inception his was to be a world-wide crusade. During 1933 the Mission received applications for four other unevangelised regions - in Colombia, Arabia, Little Tibet and Spanish Guinea - as well as the Congo. So the name of the Society was changed from "The Heart of Africa Mission" to "The World-Wide Evangelisation Crusade". All in a single year God sent along fifteen new missionaries with all the money needed for their equipment and passages - and three new fields were entered.

We were among that second group of fifteen. After Ivor Davis, the last of the ten had sailed, Fred Dunbar was number 11, Eric Smith No. 12 and I was No.13 Most of our mornings at 19 Highland Road were spent in Bible Study and prayer - praying for the money to pay for our fares and equipment. One morning while we were going through the Books of Kings and Mr. Grubb was talking about the life of faith, Colonel Munro, the WEC Treasurer, burst in to announce that money had just been received which was designated to send three new missionaries to the Congo - and there ready and waiting were the three of us. Shortly after that Colonel Munro took us along to the Army and Navy Stores in Victoria Street to be kitted out. First he bought each of us a big black tin trunk. Into it was packed khaki shorts, shirts, long socks, mosquito net, topee and all the things needed for living in the tropics. The next edition of the WEC magazine carried a photograph of the three of us in our kit under the caption "The first of the Fifteen taking shape". "Some shape!" remarked Colonel Munro.

At last things were moving - and moving quickly. We were allowed a week's home leave to say goodbye to our families. It was Easter 1933. Before we left London, Mr. Grubb said, "you must be back here by the Tuesday after the Easter Bank Holiday". For me that meant leaving Belfast on Bank Holiday Monday itself. So I asked, "please can I stay over for the Faith Mission Convention at Bangor on Easter Monday?" "No", was the firm response. Thus I went back to say farewell to my Father and Sisters and all my friends in the churches. It was then that Father gave me that set of car tools which proved so useful. As the ferry sailed down Belfast Lough we passed Bangor and I could see the Convention tent and knew that among the hundreds inside were those who were praying for me. Before the end of the week we had boarded ship at Southampton and sailed for Genoa. It was the first time I had been outside the United Kingdom - I was 24. We sailed across the Mediterranean, passed through the Suez Canal and down the Red Sea. In the distance we saw Mount Sinai. After three weeks we landed at Mombasa. During the voyage we had made a start on learning the main tribal trade language of the Ibambi region - Kingwana - a dialect of Swahili. From Mombasa we took the train to Nairobi - that railway is an amazing piece of engineering - and it was a thrill to see elephant, rhino and other African animals out in the wild. In Nairobi we stayed with the Salvation Army Commander and during our week there we met C.T. Studd's granddaughter (Alfred Buxton's daughter). Then it was on by train to Kampala in Uganda and then by road to Lake Albert. As we were boarding the steamer to cross the Lake from Uganda into the Belgian Congo we saw a man being bitten by a crocodile. On the Congo shore of the Lake we were met by Harold Williams with the WEC truck. He then drove us to the WEC field headquarters at Ibambi. This had been the last pioneering headquarters to be established by C.T. Studd - it was to reach the large Mabhudu tribe. He moved to Ibambi in August 1921 and there he died and was buried in July 1931 - and now in May 1933 there I was standing beside his grave.

Meanwhile back home in Britain, Ivy Roberts was preparing to set out for Central Africa. By May the money for her equipment and passage had come in and so she returned to Gwystre Farm to say farewell. It was a struggle to fight back the tears when she embraced her beloved parents on Leominster Station - the tears flowed once the train was on its way. Ivy was spared the knowledge that she had seen them for the last time this side of Heaven. Edith Patton (who was to become Mrs. Moules) was returning from furlough and so she accompanied Ivy on the voyage from Southampton to Mombasa. By the time they reached Ibambi, Ivy was well into Kingwana - she was always better than me at picking up languages. I was still at Ibambi, and when we met up again, the first thing Ivy said was, "aren't you thin!" For the first time (and only time until we left the Congo) I had malaria and had lost some weight.

At weekends, Mr. Harrison would take me with him when he went out to the villages. Often he would say "you give the message". Then I had to try to preach in Kingwana. After a few weeks at Ibambi, Ivy was sent to join her brother and sister at Imbai's - the station north of Wamba where, twelve years before, C.T. Studd had found a congregation of 1,500 awaiting his arrival squatting out in the open in the midday sun. There in 1925 he had built what became known as the "cricket pitch church" - a mud and thatch building 22 yards in length. Ivy was learning Kingwana so quickly that she was able to take the place of Lily Peckett (who was about to become Mrs. Frank Cripps), teaching in the girls' school and helping with the morning dispensary while continuing language study. Jack Harrison, who was our field leader, asked me to take Ivy up to Imbai's in the Mission's little Morris car - she needed help with her mountain of luggage. On the way we had to cross two rivers by pontoons - platforms built across long canoes. As I gingerly nudged the car up the planks and on to the pontoon I didn't tell Ivy that I'd never taken a vehicle on to a pontoon before.

Ivy came down to Ibambi with Jack and Lily Roberts the following Christmas for what was to become the annual field conference. The previous year a conference had been held there during the month of July on the anniversary of "Bwana's" death - then at least 7,000 Africans had attended. July was the cotton planting season so Jack Harrison decided to call the second conference at Christmas but preparations began in August. Ivor Davies was in charge of building operations and I helped him erect six large sheds each 75 feet in length. Then we constructed a large 'church' covering an area 70 yards by 30 yards - sufficient space to give shade from the sun for over 10,000 people. More than 250 African Christians volunteered to help us - thousands of bamboo poles were cut and carried from the forest and many more thousands of palm branches.

Between ten and twelve thousand Africans from eight different tribes came to the meetings. Some had walked from Poko 200 miles away, some from Kondolole had been on the road for a month. Fifty missionaries attended and Mr. and Mrs. van Staden, who were visiting from South Africa, gave the ministry. Later they described the experience as "the greatest Christmas of their lives". The local Belgian Government resident (agent) was very nervous - he thought that with such a mixture of tribes there was certain to be inter-tribal rivalry, disputes and fighting. He actually attended one of our meetings and was amazed at how peaceable and friendly everyone was - he didn't seem to be able to take it in. Although the teaching was in Kingwana (with translation into the other tribal languages) I couldn't understand much of what was said. One meeting does stand out in my memory, it ended with a huge bonfire. It was an after-meeting for leading African Christians - elders and catechists - Mr. Harrison was concerned that some of them were allowing trading activities to take priority over their Christian work, others were still addicted to tobacco, and some were smoking hemp. The Holy Spirit brought deep conviction on the meeting as Mr. Harrison spoke. Then he ordered that large banana leaves be cut and laid on the platform. An appeal was made for all those who wanted to serve God wholeheartedly to be rid of these things. From all over the gathering, men and women brought out tobacco, cigarettes and "bangi" (hemp) bringing it forward to the platform and placing it on the leaves until there was a big pile. Then it was taken outside and burnt.

Early in 1934, I was sent to our station at Wamba to work with Harold Williams and his wife and to continue language study in Kingwana. Wamba was the first station to be opened in the Ituri Forest - by James Lowder and his wife in 1920 - it was a Belgian Government "poste" - the administrative centre for the Ituri district. Mr. and Mrs. Williams were Australian - he was a chemist by profession - but Harold had been the official chauffeur in charge of the field transport since 1927 and was often away from Wamba with the lorry on transport duties. It was a privilege to spend two years with Harold Wiliams. He was always 'the willing one' - he really gave himself for God. Often he would drive all night long on some errand. Once the mission car was off the road with engine trouble when it was needed to collect some new missionaries arriving on the field. We worked for two nights and two days taking the engine out, replacing the bearings and getting it going again. Then I went to bed but Harold drove straight off - that was Harold Williams - he's with the Lord now.

However, Harold's frequent absences from Wamba meant that I had to take responsibility for the station workmens' morning Bible study - so my Kingwana rapidly improved towards the end of our first year in the Congo. This time last year we had been listening to Mr. Grubb's Bible expositions in London, now I was conducting Bible studies in the Ituri Forest in Kingwana and Ivy was teaching the schoolgirls up at Imbai's in Kingwana - but more fluently!

•••

"Then Samuel took a stone and set it between Mizpeh and Shen, and called the name of it 'Ebenezer', saying 'Hitherto hath the LORD helped us'."
1 Samuel 7 : 12

Chapter Five

Revival at Imbai's*

❖

ON THEIR RETURN FROM THE IBAMBI CONFERENCE
IN DECEMBER 1934, JACK, LILY AND IVY BECOME
conscious that the work at Imbai's was not progressing as well as it
had during the Station's first decade. Something was wrong somewhere and it must be put right. So they cancelled the usual Christmas programme and called the people to prayer. The prayer meeting was a fiasco - the hardness of heart of the congregation being
visible in their sour, sullen faces. No other meeting was announced
and the usual district conference was postponed for a week.

Jack, Lily and Ivy went to their own rooms and spent the rest of
the day alone in prayer. The next three days were given over to
prayer, and gradually a calm confidence grew that something out of
the ordinary would happen when the conference opened. The first
meeting started in the same oppressive atmosphere, Jack preached
on Acts 17 : 30 - "God commandeth all men everywhere to repent"
- and before he had finished the atmosphere had changed. At the
noon meeting he spoke again from the same text - it was five o'clock

* Much of the material in this chapter is taken from Lily Roberts's account of the revival
which was recorded by Eva Stuart Watt in "Floods on Dry Ground", published by Marshall,
Morgan and Scott in 1939.

before he stopped. At the close he said quietly, "Will those of you who want to get right with God do so now? The meeting is open for public confession of sin".

Some of the leading Christians began to confess their lack of love for God's word and for prayer and their slackness in giving. Then came a real break-through. One after another stood up and confessed to stealing - some years before, some more recently. However, compared with the Christians from the surrounding villages, the station residents were still very hard. They seemed to wince as broken, humble confessions continued around them at intervals until dusk. No one seemed to notice that it was getting dark; the congregation just sat as though glued to their seats, quite unconscious of time. At half-past six, one of the house lads slipped out and brought a lantern to the platform, and the meeting continued until ten o'clock. The people dispersed silently - even the children slipped off to bed quiet as mice. Usually at conference times everybody was very much alive with conversations lasting into the early hours of the morning. That night all was hushed at Imbai's. Satan was putting up a terrific resistance in the station's Christians. They scorned those who had made confessions, particularly when the sin confessed was one of which they themselves were guilty.

The next morning at 6.30 Jack spoke to a full congregation. Again he spoke from the text "God commandeth all men everywhere to repent". He concluded by saying that the three o'clock service would be open only to those who were right with God or willing to make things right. That afternoon numbers were very small - most of the station people were absent and there were few school children. The text was unchanged. As the service continued, a little crowd of Christians began to gather outside the church. They were trying to listen without being seen. Gradually they began to creep in and take their places with the others - and so the congregation grew by 30, 40, 50, 60. Again Jack gave an opportunity for prayer and confession - and this time the break came with the station workmen. One man admitted that he had been a source of annoyance on the station, always grumbling. Carpenters confessed that they had stolen timber, nails, screws and hinges. They knew that confession also meant restitution, but the shame and humiliation of their public confession cost them far more than any restitution.

The break-through with the station school children came last, but was just as real. Several lads owned up to stealing animals out of other lads' traps. Some older boys admitted attending pagan rituals and being guilty of impure thoughts and acts. Even little children confessed to taking and hiding food which their mother had cooked for the evening meal. With tears running down their cheeks they said, "I told mother I didn't take it, but I did". Still more surprising were the girls' confessions - painting their bodies in black, white and red as a substitute for clothes, running away from school and going to dances on the quiet.

Monday night's conference meeting brought a different relationship between the Congolese Christians and the European missionaries. Where there had been some suspicion and estrangement the wounds were healed. That invisible barrier to mutual confidence - partly racial, partly social - that spoils so much work for the Lord, was broken down. It meant that Jack could share with them that evening the burden for revival that God had laid on his heart. For many, confession and restitution had brought a sense of release and such joy. All over the station, Christians worked as they had never worked before, singing hymns from morning to night. However, many others continued to hold out, harbouring unconfessed and unforgiven sin in their hearts - they became harder than ever. A spirit of conviction had fallen on the Church at Imbai's - but that was not revival - only the gateway into it. Afterwards Jack admitted, "we failed to follow up this movement of the Spirit as we should. Instead of continuing to pray for revival, we were inclined to be satisfied with what had happened".

Then, at this critical moment, God used an unexpected crisis to complete His work. Early in 1935, the Belgian Government issued a decree limiting each missionary society to a certain number of stations according to the size of its expatriate staff. At that time our number was down to twelve. Jack Harrison called us to an emergency conference at Ibambi to decide which stations should be given up. However, the Lord showed us that this apparent set-back could be turned into an advance. If less than twelve of the existing stations were retained, then the remaining unevangelised territory in our region could be opened up. As a result, four well established stations - all close together and all among the same tribe, the Mabudus - were selected for evacuation by the missionaries, the churches and schools being left in charge of local elders, catechists and evangelists.

Imbai's was one of the four stations. When the decision was announced the Africans were shocked and disheartened. They said that Jack and Lily and Ivy couldn't really be interested in them and they wouldn't accept that they were now well able to take full responsibility for the work. Really, it was a matter of pride - they wanted the missionaries to stay because of the prestige it brought them. Furthermore, they thought they had achieved more than other stations - they were particularly proud of their huge "Garden of God". Quite voluntarily the Christians of Imbai's had cleared a large area of forest and planted it with rice. Rice takes a lot of care in growing especially when it is ripening and everyone gave one day of labour each week to the "Garden of God". Then, when the harvested rice was sold, the money was given to God's work. So they were very disgruntled; "Why close us down?" they asked.

A few months later, Jack was transferred south to join Fred Dunbar in starting up a mission station deep in the forest at Alambi among the Walesi (a pygmi tribe). "This is the beginning of the end", the Africans said, "soon the ladies will go too."

Rather than a spirit of revival, there was a spirit of rebellion on the station compound. Lily and Ivy were greatly burdened by this spiritual hardening and sense of grievance. They realised that either the work would crumble to dust as soon as the station was evacuated or - if God sent Holy Ghost revival - it would live and grow. So they stopped all their regular teaching work (Lily taught the boys' school and Ivy the girls') and gave themselves over to prayer and intercession. Many alterations were made to the station routine. Lily wrote, "Nothing really mattered except preparing to receive the best God had for us". Each day they studied the subject of the Person and work of the Holy Spirit in the Scriptures and then passed on to the Africans what they had been taught in the daily services. All the messages were on the same theme, all the praying to the same end - a Holy Ghost revival. Gradually the meetings lengthened and interest in revival increased. Christians came from long distances and a special dormitory was built for them. Most of this teaching they had heard before but the Holy Spirit was making it new to them.

A renewed conviction of sin gradually came over the congregation - particularly over their sense of grievance at the coming withdrawal of the missionaries. On leaving the church one day after hearing a message based on Galatians 2 : 20, one woman rung her hands in despair and, turning to another asked, "What are we to do? We are such terrible sinners!" One morning Lily and Ivy entered the church for the morning meeting and at first they thought there was nobody there. Then they realised that the building was full - but all the Africans were down on their knees, their faces on the seat in front, silent and broken before the Holy Presence of God. This moved them to ever more urgent prayer for spiritual deliverance and revival. Apart from the meetings and some dispensary work in the mornings, they spent all day alone with God - ordinary meals were forgotten. A few days later an unusual sense of God's Presence was felt in the morning service; and, when it was proposed to have an additional evening meeting, the congregation unanimously responded - "that's exactly what we want!" So, day after day, for eleven weeks, the meetings continued twice a day. Lily had one chapter of Scripture laid on her heart - Isaiah 58. Every morning she read it out at the service - even those who couldn't read came to know it by heart. Lily wrote, "The Lord brought me personally very low through those words, 'If thou draw out thy soul to the hungry;' that is, if I would feel their hunger, not if I would throw bread to them. I knew God had to effect this in my own heart".

Lily and Ivy became convicted of their own ill-tempered racial pride, their unconcern for souls, their lack of true worship and pure love to God. Then they too had to publicly humble themselves in brokenness and confession.

As night fell one Saturday evening and Isaiah Chapter 58 was being read to the congregation, the Holy Spirit came - as quietly as the dew, He descended upon them. The meeting had started at 6.30 p.m. - it went on until nearly midnight. One after another they cried to God in repentance, sorrow and weeping until their tears were turned to joy. In place of their sin and need, they saw the Lord Jesus Christ, and when the meeting finally closed, they went to their huts clothed with the glorious joy of the Son of God. At the Sunday service next morning they were all lifted to a higher plane of worship and praise.

During the following days Christian believers were given almost unutterable personal experiences of God's Presence which left them overflowing with joy. These believers now had a sense of the perilous state of unbelievers and of their responsibility towards them. They became concerned for their neighbours or relatives and prayed as never before for their conversion, bringing them along to the meetings. Outsiders crowded into the meetings. This resulted in conversions at almost every session - sometimes only two or three, sometimes twenty, thirty or forty.

News of the revival spread rapidly round the district. Many Africans were afraid to come to Imbai's - and even afraid of being mentioned in prayer. One afternoon, down at Wamba station, two days' journey away, the mail man arrived and saluted the missionary at the office window:

"What's the news?" asked Charlie Searle

"New news" he replied

"What's this new news?"

"News of prayer, Bwana: nothing but prayer! Everybody is praying".

"Where's that?"

"Over there at Imbai's. You come out of your hut in the morning and look around and see nothing but people praying or reading the Bible. All day they are at it!"

A few weeks later, Jack Scholes visited Imbai's - Jack Harrison had gone home on furlough and Jack Scholes had taken his place as field leader. Jack Scholes was a deeply spiritual man. Immediately he recognised that a true work of the Holy Spirit was taking place on the station.

One morning, two of the leading African evangelists came to Lily on the verandah of the mission bungalow. Speaking very shyly they began, "Every time we go to pray, we have no peace, we are so concerned about you two. God has given us a flood of blessing, but it has not been without cost to you. As soon as we kneel before God, you fill our thoughts - all the burden you have been carrying of prayer for hours for us Babudu - but we see you are not having sufficient rest or food. Would you allow us to help carry your burden by taking charge of the secular work to relieve you. We hope you will not be offended...." The obstruction which had been the original cause of the hardness and grievance on the station had been removed. In its place was spontaneous mutual sympathy between black Christians and white Christians. So the Africans took over the dispensary and schools, the station compound and the gardens.

Ivy's brother, Jack, hadn't been working among the Walesi tribe for many weeks before his health gave way and he became very ill. He had to be evacuated to Ibambi. By that time he had been on the field for nearly eight years and was due for furlough - and Lily had been there for six. Then Mr. and Mrs. Searle received a large gift of money - far more than was needed to finance their own passage back to England for furlough - so they shared it with Jack and Lily, and the four of them came home together. Before leaving, Jack made a farewell visit to Imbai's to collect his sisters - Ivy was to be assigned to another station. What a change had come over the place! Exactly a year earlier, they had been given a burden for revival - now he could see its fruits. The people were no longer despondent because their missionaries were leaving them; they had got above that. The church was packed out for their last service. Then the mission truck came to fetch Jack, Lily and Ivy. At first the crowd were silent and tearful but, as the lorry moved away, shouts began echoing through the forest - shouts of "Hallelujah! Mungu Iko!" ("Hallelujah! God reigns!") - and that was the last they heard as they left Imbai's.

The 1935 revival did not spread beyond Imbai's - but, looking back, we can see now that it prepared us for the more general revival that came in the 1950s.

•••

"And if thou draw out thy soul to the hungry, and satisfy the afflicted soul; then shall thy light rise in obscurity, and thy

darkness be as the noonday. And the LORD shall guide thee
continually, and satisfy thy soul in drought, and make fat thy
bones; and thou shalt be like a watered garden, and like a spring
of water, whose waters fail not".
Isaiah 58 : 10 & 11

Chapter Six

Wedding Drums

❖

ABOUT THREE MONTHS AFTER THE 1934 FIELD CONFER-
ENCE AT IBAMBI, MY SISTER LILY WAS OPENING THE
mail one day at Imbai's when she said to me, "Oh! There's a letter
here for you from Wamba". Never having received a letter from
Wamba I was mystified. After reading it through I said to Lily, "It's
from Robert Milliken - he says he would like to get to know me
better - but the only way he can do so is by correspondence". Lily
said, "We will have to pray about that, Ivy". Quietly I replied, "I
don't need to pray - I know!" You see, we had spent two months
living at 19, Highland Road while on the candidates' course and
knew one another pretty well. And so our courtship by correspondence began.

We only saw each other once during the year, when Bobby had
to bring some stores up to Imbai's, but that was the year of the revival and I was busy with our work on the station. Our next meeting
was at the week-long annual field conference at Ibambi at the end of
1935. I came down to see my brother Jack who was very ill and
Bobby was helping to look after him. They were sharing a room in

the new Bible School - their room was a book store most of the time. It was at this conference that we announced our engagement. The policy of WEC was that a couple had to be on the field for two years before they could get engaged and then another two years before they could get married - and they had to be located at separate stations. Well, we fulfilled these requirements - and were content to do so.

After the 1935 conference, Jack and Lily went home on furlough and I was transferred from Imbai's to Nala further north. As part of the new mission strategy, Bobby had been designated to start a work among the Ababua tribe in the Lower Welle Province in the far north west of WEC's region. Contacts had been made with the tribe as far back as 1921 when A.W. Ruscoe, then based at Poko, had wanted to open a station at Korosa. The Ababua had had contact with Roman Catholic missionaries and were one of the most advanced and intelligent tribes in our field. So I was sent to Nala to learn Bangala (or Lingala as it is better known nowadays) which was the trade language of the Welle Provinces, while Bobby went to Egbita to do the same. Nala was one of the original three concessions occupied by C.T. Studd and Alfred Buxton in 1916 (the others were Niangara and Poko). Egbita was a more recent - and more difficult - station. Difficult because the local Paramount Chief had made a profession of faith but then, through his hopeless entanglements with his 400 'wives', had backslidden and his life had ended tragically in drink and disgrace. For six months, Bobby was the only white missionary in Egbita. The elder of the church there - a godly old white-haired man named Salomona - was his teacher and guide. In that situation Bobby picked up Bangala very quickly - he had to!

Once he had mastered the language, Bobby was released to go on trek among the villages of the Ababua tribe. He rode between the villages on a bike covering about twenty miles in a day. Along the way he would stop and talk to passers-by while his carriers had a rest. The headman of each village would provide young men to carry your camping gear - camp bed, folding chair, cooking utensils, etc. - but you had to pay them the official rate set by the Belgian authorities. Every village had a guest hut. The Africans were always very friendly and hospitable. When you arrived in a village, the headman would order someone to remove any hunting nets or other gear that was stored in the hut and clean it up, and then it was yours for as long as you wished to stay. Bobby usually stayed in each village a couple of weeks teaching the Gospel very simply, usually through hymns and choruses which could be learned by heart. Alfred Buxton had translated most of the New Testament into Bangala but, of course, these village people couldn't read.

By now Jack Scholes and the other senior missionaries were wanting to make a start on this new work among the Ababua, so - towards the end of 1936 - Jack came up to Egbita to collect Bobby in the Mission's little Morris car and take him on to Poko, which was to be his base while measuring out the new station's territorial concession. Frank and Lily Cripps took over from him at Egbita. Poko is on the banks of the wide Bomokandi River. It was there that C.T. Studd held the first baptismal service in 1921 - 147 Africans were baptised in the river - even though it's full of crocodiles!

When A.W. Ruscoe first proposed to establish a work among the Ababua in the early 1920's he was keen that the mission station should be sited at Korosa, ten kilometres north of the river Bomokandi, because he had received such a friendly reception there when on trek - but the Congolese were always friendly towards Westerners. However, it was generally assumed that our station would be there - even though there wasn't a church at Korosa and it would mean employing pagans to build it. As Harold Williams and Bobby were surveying the territory occupied by the Ababua and measuring out the proposed concession, they became conscious that the tribe occupied a far larger area than had been thought. They drove up to the nearest Norwegian Baptist Mission station at Bili and found that it was 200 kilometers from their concession to Korosa. The Norwegians told them where the south-eastern boundary of their work lay and it was agreed that the area for which W.E.C. would be responsible would begin five miles east of Buta. Bobby thought that the site of the new station should be further north nearer the centre of the concession but he began building-work at Korosa as instructed by the field council - hiring workmen, clearing ground and building a little mud and thatch house with a grass roof for us to live in after we were married. Meanwhile, the Mission had agreed that we could marry as soon as everything was settled at Korosa.

Then, when everything was finalised, the Paramount Chief at Korosa - under the influence of the Roman Catholic priests - refused to sign the concession document. The Roman Catholics had told him not to show any favour to Protestants because Belgium was a Catholic country and he would be in trouble with the Belgian Government. Bobby had just finished measuring off the compound at Korosa accompanied by the local Belgian official when the Chief refused to sign over the concession - and the Belgian official wouldn't intervene. Well, that confirmed to us that the station should be elsewhere - but what were we to do in the meantime? I was at Nala where there were only single missionaries and they needed a married couple and Bobby had returned to Wamba, but we didn't want to be based in either Nala or Wamba. Eventually Jack Scholes and the field council agreed that we could begin village work among the Ababua, itinerating from village to village without first setting up a central mission station - that could come later. I was the first lady missionary to be permitted to live such a gypsy sort of life. So now we were free to get married.

When Jack and Lily went home on furlough we had just become engaged. Since none of the 'trimmings' for a European-style wedding could be obtained in our part of the Congo, we left them to get the essentials at home and send them out to us. For example, they measured my finger before they left and then had the ring made in England. Lily was skilled at all forms of dressmaking and needlecraft - when she lived with us at Gwystre Farm she used to make a lot of the younger childrens' clothes. So naturally I asked her to make my wedding dress. Apparently she made a most beautiful dress for me - but I never saw it. You see it was taken up to London along with our wedding cake, some presents and other items to WEC headquarters for despatch to Africa, but a mistake was made, and the box was sent to the Ivory Coast instead of the Congo! Weeks after the wedding we received a letter from some WEC missionaries in the Ivory Coast thanking us for the wedding cake and saying how much they'd enjoyed it! No doubt they made good use of the wedding dress too - everything is useful on a mission station in the tropics. Well, at least the ring arrived safely.

We were to be married at Wamba where Albert and Olive Moore were now in charge because Harold Williams and his wife were back in Australia on furlough. Albert and Olive were already engaged when they came out to the Congo and they had recently been married on the field. Olive still had her wedding dress and since we were about the same size, I tried it on - it fitted - and so we thanked God for His providence.

On March 19th 1938 I stopped being Ivy Roberts and became Ivy Milliken. It was a very full day. First there had to be the civil ceremony at the "poste" in Wamba to comply with Belgian law. This was conducted in French by the Belgian resident with our field leader, Jack Harrison and his wife acting as witnesses. Then there was the African Christian ceremony in our church at Wamba. The church was packed out - over a thousand Africans attended the service which was conducted by Jack Harrison in Kingwana. Afterwards all the school boys lined up outside the church and we paraded down through the avenue. In the evening we had a third service with the other missionaries in the mission bungalow in English. It was then that Bobby gave me the wedding ring that had been sent out from England - inscribed inside it are the words: "Holiness unto the Lord". We had invited the Belgians along to the bungalow for this service and to the reception afterwards - six officials wearing full uniform came with their wives. Three ceremonies in one day and a reception. We were well and truly married!

•••

"Two are better than one ... and a threefold cord is
not quickly broken."
Ecclesiastes 4 : 9 - 12

The church Bobby and Ivy pastored in Courrières, France.

Bobby and Ivy on their 50th Wedding Anniversary.

Chapter Seven

First-Fruits

---------------------------- ❖ ----------------------------

AFTER OUR WEDDING AT WAMBA JACK SCHOLES TOOK
US UP TO POKO. THERE WE LEFT OUR HEAVY LUGGAGE.
The local Greek trader regularly travelled the road between Poko,
Buta and Stanleyville and we persuaded him to take us and the rest
of our baggage up to the furthest village in our area. Bunia was
about 300 kilometres from Poko - an Ababua chief lived there. Here
our five years of gypsy life itinerating around the villages began. As
we were leaving Poko, Jack Scholes said to us, "I believe you are
going to have a good response among the Ababua because my Mother
has been praying for twenty years that missionaries will be sent to
that tribe". Prayer is of tremendous benefit. I believe it was through
Mrs. Scholes' prayers in Liverpool that the people were prepared to
receive the Gospel.

A few weeks after our arrival in Bunia we met Bati - the head
man of the neighbouring village of Pamir. He said, "Please come
and teach in my village - I'll build you a house". So we moved
down to Pamir which was the cleanest, best organised village in the
district. The hut that Bati had built for us was so neat and tidy that

the Belgian officials preferred it to their own official guest huts when on tours of inspection. Bati had been a sergeant in the Congolese army so he was more familiar with the ways of the outside world, he could read and he wasn't a polygamist. On one occasion, when serving in the army, he had passed through Deti where Lilian Dennis had been in charge of our station on Deti Hill since 1929. Bati had attended the church and met Miss Dennis who explained the Gospel to him. Later he told us that at the time he had said to himself, "If I get an opportunity, the first missionary I meet I'm going to ask him to come to my village".

We stayed in Pamir for several months teaching the villagers Christian choruses and hymns - they learnt them very quickly - Africans have excellent retentive memories. Bati was one of the first to profess faith in Christ and be baptised. From then on right down through the years he lived a consistent committed Christian life out and out for the Lord. We trained him to be a catechist and he became the leader of the church in Pamir. What a marvellous response there was in that village! Every morning at 6 o'clock the Christians paraded - I had the men, Ivy had the boys and the wives of the Christian men. Ivy trained two older boys as monitors to help her with their class. They were taught to read and write and there was a brief Christian message each morning. That was from 6 o'clock until 7, and then from 7 a.m. until 8 a.m., I taught the men Christian doctrine and practice from the Scriptures training them to go out into surrounding villages as catechists. When there were sufficient converts in a village the Christians would obtain permission from the head man to build a little church for their meetings. During the day the Africans would be out of the village working in their gardens or on the plantations and then we would go around the huts talking to the grannies who were left to look after the very young children. In the evening we talked with the villagers around the communal fire (its purpose was to keep wild animals away at night - not to keep them warm!) and it was then that we taught them simple hymns and choruses - Ivy accompanying them on her concertina. All of this was, of course, in the Bangala language - which is a good teaching medium.

From Pamir we went to Yema and from Yema to Komo and from there to Sombo and from there to Malingwia, working along the motor road which ran all the way from the Sudanese border down through Niangara to Buta and on to Stanleyville. We stayed a couple of months in each village but when the time came to move on the people never wanted us to leave. We assured them we would be back and told the local catechists to carry on with the work.

Another very fruitful village was Komo. This was a plantation village with four large coffee plantations nearby. Within a few weeks of our arrival a good number of plantation workers had professed conversion, and soon a congregation had been formed and active outreach begun. The plantations were owned by Belgian or Portuguese expatriates. One of them was run by a Belgian named Monsieur Fontaine - his wife was actually French and a nominal Protestant at that. Madame Fontaine always made us very welcome, she was interested in our work at Komo and eventually had her two daughters and two sons dedicated in our church. When the War came she volunteered for work in the Government offices in Stanleyville, but she kept in touch with us and invited us to stay with her when we passed through Stanleyville on our way home on furlough.

Perhaps the most successful work of all was at Sombo - named after the local river - which was the village where the brothers Palangi, Dudu and Edidi lived. They were three great hefty hearty fellows - all the children of the same mother and father and all natural leaders. When we first met them they drank heavily (Edidi was a real drunkard - his brothers always said that one day a leopard would get him), they smoked hemp, were deeply involved in witchcraft and practised polygamy - Palangi had seven wives, Dudu five, and Edidi three. Those three brothers just loved singing the hymns and choruses in the evening after they had come in from the cotton fields. Through frequent repetition they learned the Gospel. When the time came for us to move on to Malingwia they pleaded with us to stay and teach them more songs but we felt we should keep to our itinerary. After we left Sombo, Edidi (the youngest and boldest of the brothers) continued to sing the songs and choruses around the village fire each evening and out in the fields. One day the local Roman Catholic priest heard him and determined to put a stop to it. So he went to the local paramount chief - Aponda - and said, "This fellow, Edidi, is going to get you a bad name with the Belgians he's promoting these Protestants and you will lose favour". The priest urged chief Aponda to make an example of Edidi and put him in prison. We had just moved down to Malingwia when we received a message that Edidi was in prison for singing our gospel hymns. So I immediately cycled back to the chief's village and demanded, "Why have you put Edidi in prison?" Aponda replied, "Oh, Bwana, I don't want any trouble with you or anybody - the priest asked me to do it". So I said, "Well I'm going straight to the Belgian Government official at Titule". Aponda said "Oh, Bwana, Bwana, don't make a fuss - I'll let him go". The chief could see that he was being used by the Roman Catholics so he released Edidi.

When Edidi got back to Sombo he said,

"We don't want anything to do with those priests. We want to become your people".

That gave me the opportunity to impress on them what being God's true Christian children entailed. I said,

"Are you willing to give up all your drinking and hemp smoking? You know it's not good for you".

They said "We are".

"Are you willing to give up witchcraft? You know it's not good for you".

They said "We are".

"Are you willing to give up polygamy? You know how much trouble you have with all these wives. Because they are treated like slaves by the head wife to work your cotton fields they keep running away. They are jealous and they quarrel among themselves and they don't love you."

They said, "You are absolutely right. We have got more trouble with these women than its worth".

So I read Genesis chapter 2 and explained that God intended that a man should only have one wife. When they agreed to give up their polygamous marriages we agreed to come back to Sombo for one more month. During that month all three brothers were soundly converted. From then on they set the standard for the whole of our work in that district. If we had been weak with them on these matters the work would never have been established at Sombo. At Pamir, Bati wasn't a polygamist, neither were the church leaders on the coffee plantations at Komo, so these problems didn't arise there.

Those three brothers became stalwart Christians - marvellous trophies of God's grace. They were so keen - they quickly learned to read Bangala and soon were leading a great work at Sombo. Eventually (when we were serving our second term on the field) Dudu and Edidi went to Ibambi Bible School to train as pastors - and for that they had to learn Kingwana first. Palangi remained as catechist of the church at Sombo. During the Simba Uprising in the 1960's Dudu was martyred - but I'll tell you more about him in a later chapter. All three brothers are in Heaven now - and so is Bati.

We were also able to establish a fruitful work at Malingwia which was just up the road from the Government "poste" at Titule. The village was in a fine situation with good water and plenty of wood available. Above all it was in a central position about 100 kilometres east of Buta and about the same distance west of Niangara. By contrast there was virtually no response at Korosa - the intended mission centre - we called it "the cement district" because of its spiritual hardness. Gradually we became convinced that the principal mission station for work among the Ababua should be sited at Malingwia.

It was the usual practice among missionaries to take on a "house boy" to do household chores like washing and cooking. They supervised the transport of our two camp beds, two camp chairs, two suitcases, boxes of cooking utensils and crockery, and were a great help to us when we were busy teaching. These house boys would be young African Christians with obvious aptitude for training as future leaders of the Congolese Church. Apart from the Biblical and spiritual teaching they gained from living with us, they would be given a good domestic training and were paid the amount the Belgian Government stipulated. Often the Belgians would come to us saying, "Could we have some of the house boys you have trained because they are well trained and trustworthy".

Soon after we began itinerating around the villages Mattiasi (Matthew) was brought to us by his Mother who was a Christian. She was also a leper and dared not keep him with her any longer, and so we brought him up until he went to Bible College. Mattiasi's Mother gave us money to buy him a Bangala Bible. He always kept that Bible with him stuck in the back pocket of his shorts. Whenever he had a spare moment he pulled it out and read it. By the time we were able to go on furlough Mattiasi had grown physically and spiritually and was well grounded in the Scriptures. We took him to Ibambi and he entered the Bible School to be trained as an evangelist. God greatly used Mattiasi during the Revival in the 1950s. His spiritual maturity enabled him to keep the meetings steady and restrain those who would resort 'to the flesh'. Only recently (March 1994) we received a letter from him. Of course, he is now an elderly man - he's been Pastor of the Protestant Church in Malingwia for many years and is renowned for his knowledge of the Scriptures.

I suppose it must have been in the year 1940 that Jack and Lily returned from furlough because the book, "Floods on Dry Ground" came out in 1939. While he was in England Jack had become engaged to Olive Rodgers who was from Leominster and a close friend of his sister Daisy. Olive came out to the Congo in 1945 and they were married at Malingwia. Jack and Lily joined us in the work among the Ababua and they too found our method of travelling around the villages using their guest huts as bases to be effective. After a while we divided the area into three sectors - we worked one, Lily another, and Jack a third - each of us teaching for several weeks in each village in our sector - with remarkable results. By this time the war in Europe had been underway for a year or more. It had been going for six months before we knew anything about it - there were no newspapers or radios where we were. One day we met a distraught official whose family was back in Belgium and he told us that the Germans had invaded his country.

In 1941 Jack wrote home, 'We four are the only missionaries among more than 100,000 people. From here to our nearest mission station is 270 miles. I am in a house by a railway line. If I work down this line for 120 miles among the densely populated villages, I shall be the first ever to preach the Gospel to them.'

It was in the March of that year that our daughter, Joy, was born. We went back to Poko for the last weeks of Ivy's pregnancy because there was a Belgian doctor in Poko and Muriel Harman - a Canadian nurse / midwife - was teaching at our station there. Muriel had come out to Congo with the Heart of Africa Mission back in 1926 - she delivered all the missionaries' babies - and she delivered Joy on March 22nd. Twenty years later Muriel was murdered by the Simbas.

I never had malaria after that first bout at Ibambi in 1933 but Ivy frequently suffered from malarial fever. These recurring attacks would leave her weak and listless. Soon after Joy's first birthday Ivy suffered such a bad attack of malaria that we had to go down to Poko as the Belgian doctor was still there.

While Ivy recovered I was helping with the building of a new brick church. One day Joy was sleeping out on the verandah in the cot I had made for her. As I walked by I noticed that a large black fly had got under the mosquito net and was on Joy's lip. Quickly I brushed it off - but a day or so later Joy became very ill. We took her to the doctor but he didn't seem to know how to treat her. Jack Scholes suggested that we take her down to Ibambi in the mission van. Joy's condition was deteriorating. She became very dehydrated and by the time we reached Ibambi she was like a lifeless limp doll. Our field leader, Jack Harrison, suggested that we take her on to Nebobongo where Percy and Edith Moules were just establishing their leprosarium. They had studied for a diploma at the Belgian School of Tropical Medicine while they were on furlough in 1939. As we got back into the van Jack quietly asked, "Are you ready to lose her, Brother?"

Nebobongo is only a short distance from Ibambi. Mrs. Moules immediately took our little girl, examined her, and detected a slight pulse. Then she gave her an injection of saline solution - Joy didn't move a muscle when the needle went in. Several more injections followed in rapid succession until it took both Percy and me to hold her still. Edith told us that had we arrived an hour later it would have been too late. Within a couple of weeks Joy was 'as right as rain'. Percy's comment was, "We have seen many wonderful things here - but this is the first resurrection."

By 1942 we had been travelling around the villages for five years. All over the region little congregations of Christians were springing up and the congregation at Sombo were pressing us to establish a proper school. We said, "Well, you pray that God will get us permission to build a mission station - and you must be ready to help build it". The Lord answered their prayers in a marvellous way. A new Belgian administrator was appointed to the area and he took an interest in our work. One day he said to us, "Why don't you build churches in your villages like the Catholics do in theirs?" Then I explained that the Paramount Chief had refused us permission to build. He replied, "Oh I'll see to that. You just write out applications for the places where you want churches and send them to me. I'll take them to the Chief and I'll see that he signs them". That was the first break-through. Later he asked, "Why don't you build a mission station?" Exactly what the people had been praying for. So we made application through this official to build a station at Malingwia.

From the outset the project was completely indigenous. The Africans had approached us to set up the station, they prayed for it, they financed it - and they built it. While we were waiting for permission to come through from Stanleyville the African Christians gave tithes of the proceeds from the sale of their cotton to finance the project, and they asked me to be their treasurer. By the time we received permission from the Belgians to build the station at Malingwia it was possible to get back to England for furlough - we had been away eleven years. Our Field Council agreed to Jack and Lily's request that they should carry on our work at Malingwia and I handed over the funds to Jack. Before we left for our first furlough twenty young Christian couples (including Palangi, Dudu, and Edidi and their wives) had volunteered to build the station - and we had measured out the concession.

Thus, during our first term of service, God used us to establish a new approach to church-planting and a new Mission policy. Through starting in the villages, establishing congregations and building churches in villages where there was a response to the Gospel, and only then (if requested) building a central mission station, the work of WEC in the Congo began to take a new direction. Of course we were only developing a work begun by others twenty years before. By translating the Scriptures and hymn book into Bangala C.T. Studd, Alfred Buxton and Norman Grubb had given us the tools with which to carry on the job. Before we went on furlough the method we had pioneered had been successfully adopted by Aubrey Brown at Kesanga and Fred Dunbar at Kondolole.

During our first five years among the Ababua tribe, we had witnessed hundreds of conversions, the gathering of more than a dozen congregations of believers in as many villages, the building of seven churches, and start on the construction of a central mission station at Malingwia.

To God be the glory.

•••

"Now unto Him that is able to do exceeding abundantly above all that we ask or think, according to the power that worketh in us; Unto Him be glory in the church by Christ Jesus throughout all ages, world without end Amen."
Ephesians 3: 20 & 21.

Grandson Mark's Wedding.
From left to right: Bobby (Jnr), Karen, Kevin, Thane, Karen, Mark, Joy,
Vivian, Christine, Corin and Bobby

Farewell service at Courrières, France.

Chapter Eight

Going Home

❖

EARLY IN 1944 WE STARTED TO PREPARE FOR FURLOUGH.
AS WE LOOKED BACK OVER THE YEARS TO OUR ARRIVAL
in north-east Congo in 1933 we could see that it had been a decade
of great change. The Belgian Government had taught and encouraged the Africans to grow cotton for export and then built a motor
road right through the region. The soil was very fertile. So the
Africans were already self-sufficient in food grown in their gardens
(and they kept chickens & goats - and they still went hunting - on
Saturdays!). Now they were growing a cash crop so they had money
to spend. The Greek traders sold them bicycles, sewing machines
and European cloth. When we first arrived the women wore simple
bark-cloth skirts and the men next-to-nothing; now the men were
buying European clothes from the Greeks and the women wore very
attractive colourful print dresses. About 2 months earlier I was
preaching at Komo on the text "Peace through the blood of Christ"
(Colossions 1 v 20) - Madame Fontaine was there in the service.
Although Tata couldn't read or write, he was a very alert wise old
man. He advised the Chief when there were disputes to be sorted

out in the villages or at the Chief's court. Tata was greatly respected. Anyway, while I was preaching on the blood of Christ, the light suddenly broke into his heart and mind - he saw it in a flash. He jumped up and said,

"Bwana, sit down. I have understood what you are trying to tell us and I will explain it to my people".

He turned to them and said,

"Years ago, when we Ababua were pagans and cannibals and always fighting against the Bazande and wanted to make peace we took a slave from some other tribe, sacrificed him, and took his blood to make peace. Now I can understand what a wonderful thing we are hearing tonight - God wants to make peace with us through the blood of His Son - even though we are rebels and sinners against Him".

Then Tata confessed,

"I have been a very bad man, but I want to have that peace. I don't want to die as an enemy of God with sin in my heart. So after the meeting I am going to talk to the missionary".

When the people had dispersed we spent a long time with dear Tata explaining the way of salvation and then he prayed and asked God to give him that "peace through the blood." Do you know he came right through - he was gloriously saved.

Tata couldn't read or write - but he opened up several villages for us. Everywhere he went he would sing and then teach the villagers the Gospel from memory.

We had told Tata that we were expecting to go home to England shortly. Then he became ill and asked me to come and see him. He was radiant - he did have "that peace of God that passeth all understanding". Tata said, "I know I'm going to Heaven. I know my sins have been forgiven. I want you to bury me and I want you to tell the people there's to be no witchdoctor because I'm going to be with the Lord Jesus in Heaven". In pagan funerals the mourners cut themselves and call upon the witchdoctors to find out who has bewitched the deceased and cause them to die - they don't believe in a natural death. Tata said "I don't believe in that now. I'm going to be with the Lord. So get the Christians to come and sing - and get them to sing my favourite hymn - 'I am so glad that our Father in Heaven'".

He died a few hours later. His sons made his coffin and he was buried the next day. What a tremendous testimony to God's saving grace! Tata died in the Lord. His cheerful, Christian funeral was a great witness to the Ababua people.

Before we left Malingwia the concession had been granted, the forest cleared, and Jack had made a start on constructing the station buildings. There was to be a church, a school, staff bungalows, huts for the boys of Christian parents, and huts for the widows who were to look after the girls. We planned for a hundred school boys and fifty school girls. The buildings that Jack supervised were made of the traditional materials - mud, sticks, thatch and grass - but the Africans gave me money to buy a brick-making machine in Stanleyville so that eventually the station would have more permanent buildings.

After weeks of anticipation our departure for our first furlough came very suddenly. One day in March Harold Williams arrived in Malingwia with the mission truck (he had driven through the night) and the next night he took us off to Wamba, where we were to await the weekly mail van which would take us to Stanleyville. Joy had her third birthday while we were waiting in Wamba. We hadn't been able to buy Joy any toys or dolls while we were up in the Ababua villages, she had to make do with what I could make. In place of a doll Joy had a young pigeon. Bati had given it to her when it was a chick and she kept it and cuddled it and always had it with her - but she kept it wrapped up so tightly that it never learned to fly. When we came away from Malingwia she insisted on bringing it with us. There was a Norwegian missionary staying at Wamba when we were there. 'When he saw Joy cuddling this pigeon he went straight out to a shop which was run by Dutch people and bought her a Dutch doll as a birthday present. Only then was she willing to leave her pigeon behind with one of the African Christians at Wamba. It never did learn to fly. When we passed through Wamba on our way back from furlough it was still there. Actually Joy nearly lost her Dutch doll. When we were on the boat another little girl in a fit of jealousy snatched it from her and threw it over the railing. How Joy did yell! Mercifully we were on the top deck at the time - I dashed down the stairs and found it lying in a life-boat.

My only memory of our long trip by road from Wamba to Stanleyville was one night when we suddenly came across a troop of baboons, their eyes shining in the headlamps. In the darkness the mail van ran into them and one was killed. The driver stopped, picked up the dead baboon, and casually remarked, "We'll have baboon soup tonight!" When we reached Stanleyville we were overwhelmed by the sight of so much traffic and bustle. Joy was terrified by the traffic. I had to carry her everywhere.

We had to wait a week for the boat that would take us down the Congo River to Leopoldville and had accepted Madame Fontaine's long-standing invitation to stay with her. While I was there I bought the brick-making machine and arranged to collect it on our return. Then Ivy received a telegram from England. It was from Daisy. Their Mother had passed away suddenly at Gwystre Farm even as we were on our way home. So I've yet to meet my Mother-in-law - but I'll meet her in Heaven.

The voyage between Stanleyville and Leopoldville down the Congo takes a week. The steamer only travels during the day - at night it ties up at jetties along the banks of the River. On the boat we met the Belgian officer who was in charge of the Salvation Army work in the Congo and his wife - Colonel and Mrs. Becket. The Salvation Army was opening up new missions in the towns along the Congo River. Colonel and Mrs. Becket had just started a new corps in Stanleyville and were returning to Salvation Army Headquarters. They invited us to stay with them until we were given permission to travel down to the coast. We were in Leopoldville for three weeks, and we were able to help the Beckets with meetings at the citadel.

At last we were allowed to take the ferry across the river to Brazzaville in the French Congo. From there we caught a train which took us down to the port of Pointe Noire - and there an ocean-going liner was in dock ready to sail to England. It was so refreshing to be beside the sea - we hadn't seen the sea for eleven years.

Normally it was a three-week voyage between Pointe Noire and Liverpool but the War was still on. First we had to sail round West Africa to Dakar in Senegal where a convoy of ships was gathering. We were on a Belgian liner. Originally it had been one of a fleet of five - but the other four had been sunk by German submarines. Blackout had to be strictly maintained throughout the voyage. Below decks it was stiflingly hot at night with curtains pulled and port holes shut. Joy suffered from terrible prickly heat rash - we used all the powder we could lay our hands on. It was a relief to be able to get up on deck where there was a breeze.

We waited at Dakar until sixty ships had arrived and the convoy had been formed. Then we sailed in formation escorted by a British aircraft carrier and several frigates that bustled around the outside like sheepdogs. We took a zig-zag route up and across the Atlantic to avoid detection by a submarine. Every ship maintained the same speed and position in the formation, always the same distance apart, all sixty ships sailing steadily along. It was a magnificent sight. When we went on deck in the morning the same ships would be in exactly the same positions around us as they had been when we went below the night before. There were several other Congo missionaries going on much-delayed furloughs like ourselves - Mr. and Mrs. Ivimey of the B.M.S. and several members of the R.B.M.U. All the men had to take turns at look-out duty at night - which I greatly enjoyed because it was much cooler up on deck. Instead of three weeks the voyage lasted six but it passed without incident and, once we had left the tropics, it became more like a pleasant holiday cruise. Everybody's health improved in the bracing sea air - especially Ivy who had been much weakened by her frequent malaria attacks. We spent as long on deck as possible. As we neared Britain we sailed out into the Atlantic and round the West coast of Ireland and then round Malin Head and into the North Channel. As we sailed passed Port Stewart a fellow Ulsterman remarked that the Port Stewart Convention was under way. It reminded me of the first stage of my journey out to Africa eleven years earlier when the ship sailed down Belfast Lough passed the Bangor Convention tent.

It was June 1944 when we arrived back in Britain - just after 'D-Day'. Our ship docked in Liverpool just as the workers were streaming out of their factories and offices for their lunch break. We were overwhelmed by all the noise and activity, and Joy was amazed to see so many people. She couldn't get over the way in which their houses were "all stuck together" in rows. The only houses she had known were the African detached huts spread out in forest clearings. Then we got off the boat and on to the train for London. When the train arrived in London it was chaotic - the Germans had just started sending over the V.1 rocket bombs - they kept coming over day and night. We managed to reach Headquarters in Upper Norwood. Mr. and Mrs. Grubb were there. They told us they were having a bad time with the bombing - "As soon as you've all seen the doctor for a check-up you must get out of London". That evening we were upstairs with Mr. Grubb when suddenly he said, "There's one coming!" From the window we watched it approaching high in the sky. Then the engine cut out, down came the rocket, there was a tremendous explosion, we could see the cloud of dust rising from where it had fallen but Joy slept through it all.

The next morning a Greek student who was staying at Headquarters drove us in the Mission's car to Harley Street where a specialist examined us - Joy yelled so much that he said she must be all right. He said that all we needed was to rest somewhere away from London. We were already on our way - our baggage was in the car - and the student took us straight on to Paddington Station. It was chaotic. When we bought our tickets we were told to get on the first train that came in and it would take us somewhere out of London in the general direction that we wanted to go. Well, we wanted to go to Leominster where Daisy and her husband Fred lived. That first train could have been going anywhere - Plymouth, Penzance, Cardiff or even back to Birkenhead - but its destination was Shrewsbury - exactly where we wanted to go. We had not been allowed to telephone to say where we were because of the war-time restrictions on passing information. So Daisy and Fred had no idea that we'd even left Africa. They were aware that we were due home on furlough and that was all. When we got to Shrewsbury we were able to telephone from the station. At first Daisy couldn't understand who it could possibly be - she had no idea we were in England. At last she said, "Well, where are you?" Ivy replied "We're at Shrewsbury Station. We're catching the next train to Leominster. We'll be with you in an hour". "Oh," she said, "Fancy that".

Now I'm going to tell you of a remarkable instance of God's leading. That very morning (June 20th) Daisy - as was her custom -

was reading "Daily Light". The text for that morning is Exodus 2.v.9 - "Take this child away and nurse it for me ...", the story of Moses' Mother and the Egyptian princess. As Daisy read that Scripture it came right home to her heart - so much so that she called her husband and read it to him. She said, "Fred, it's marvellous how God looked after that baby through the princess. Now if Ivy and Bob were here we could care for Joy in the same way that Moses was cared for". They had a son about eleven years old and they knew that if we returned to the Congo we might have to leave Joy behind, but we had never mentioned the subject to them. Well, that conversation took place in the morning Daisy thinking we were in Africa. We arrived a few hours later. That evening, as she was bathing Joy, Daisy told us of her experience in the morning and how she had responded "Lord, if Bob and Ivy were here I know it would be Joy". God's guidance was just so clear - and Joy did take to her Aunty Daisy. From then on she never left Leominster. When we went on deputation ministry Joy remained with Daisy and Fred - the Lord had provided a home for her. Earlier that day, when we arrived at Leominster, Fred and Daisy met us at the station. Daisy asked,

"Did you receive my telegram about Mum's passing?"

Ivy said, "We read it in Stanleyville. How's Dad managing?"

Quietly Daisy replied, "He's gone home with Mother to be with the Lord. The funeral was last week".

So it was with a mixture of joy and sorrow, weeping and rejoicing that we "came home again to Wales".

•••

"Jesus answered... I go to prepare a place for you. And if I go and prepare a place for you, I will come again, and receive you unto myself; that where I am, there ye may be also."
John 14: 2 & 3.

The White House
Washington

We are delighted to congratulate you on your anniversary. As you celebrate the memories of your wedding day and your life together, we know how you cherish the love that has united you through the years. At this special time we wish you every happiness and send our best wishes. May God bless you always.

Nancy Reagan

Ronald Reagan

50th Wedding greeting from President and Mrs. Ronald Regan.

Chapter Nine

First Furlough

❖

THE W.E.C. ALLOWED US SIX MONTHS COMPLETE REST BEFORE WE BEGAN DEPUTATION MINISTRY. THESE months we spent with Fred and Daisy Gurney in Leominster. Daisy's husband was manager of Leominster Co-op and they lived in a large flat above the shop where there was sufficient room for us. Just before we left the Congo the Belgian Government had passed a law which meant that in future only properly ordained ministers would be permitted to work in the country as missionaries. Most of my time in Leominster was spent studying for the ordination exam of the F.I.E.C. (Fellowship of Independent Evangelical Churches). Early in 1945 I went up to London, was examined by a committee of ministers, and came back with a Certificate of Ordination.

Joy had settled so happily with Fred and Daisy that we decided to leave her with them when we went on deputation. Mr. Grubb had asked us to accompany him on a tour of Ireland and before we left we wanted to give Joy an early birthday present. On the boat over she had been greatly taken by the red shoes another little girl was wearing. When we asked her what she would like for her birthday the answer was, of course, a pair of red shoes. Well, we hunted round every shoe shop in Leominster - and there seemed to be a lot of them - without success. We tried to persuade Joy to have some nice shoes of a different colour, but no they had to be red, nothing else would do. In the last shop we visited the manager thought that he had a pair of girls' red shoes in stock but couldn't find them. Little Joy piped up, "I'll wait until you find them". We had just got back home feeling frustrated and exhausted when the phone rang. It was the shoe shop manager - he had found a pair of red shoes under the counter. Back we went to the shop. They fitted her exactly. Exultantly Joy said, "There you are. I told you. There was a red pair for me". Over the years I've recounted that story many times as an illustration of persistency in prayer.

We explained to Joy that we were going away for some weeks but she was so happy with her Aunty Daisy and so pleased hopping and skipping around the flat in her red shoes that she didn't seem to mind at all. We set off with Mr. Grubb for Belfast and from there we went all round Ireland - North and South - all over. After six weeks we returned to Belfast only to learn that Miss Mitchell - an ex-Congo missionary who was in charge of our regional headquarters in Belfast (the Congolese called her "Ma Mi") - had to go into hospital. Mr. Grubb considered the situation and then asked us if we would stay on in Belfast and take charge of the Headquarters until Miss Mitchell had recovered from her operation. We agreed thinking it would be for only a few weeks. In the event we were in Ireland for six months - and they turned out to be very fruitful months.

We stayed in the regional Headquarters - a large house on the Antrim Road - quite close to my old home. Ivy got to know my Father and Sisters quite well. We assisted Mr. and Mrs. Johnson the leaders of The Welcome Mission. They had been very good friends ever since my conversion when a teenager. The Lord enabled us to establish several new prayer batteries - one I particularly remember was organised by the Munn sisters and held in a room above their shop. Occasionally we attended the Methodist Church but things had changed there. Faithful Gospel ministry was now looked down upon as old fashioned; modern liberal teaching dominated the pulpit - and the Church had died spiritually. The Sunday after we moved into our Belfast Headquarters I was asked to take a morning service there (the minister was unwell). I expected to have a reunion with Bob Snoddon at the church but to my surprise he wasn't among the congregation. Straight after the service I went round to his house to find out what was wrong. When he saw who was standing on the doorstep he looked very uneasy. It was past midday but clearly he had only just got out of bed - a Sunday newspaper lay open on the table. "What's this, Bobby?" I asked. Shamefaced he admitted that he didn't often go to church now. He had no desire to attend. After we had talked a while Bob agreed to come with me that evening to The Welcome Mission. From then on Bob Snoddon and his wife regularly attended The Welcome! As Mr. and Mrs. Johnson grew older so Mr. and Mrs. Snoddon helped them more and more with the work of the Mission. Eventually Mrs. Johnson died (she had been a pilgrim with the Faith Mission in her younger days). Mr. Johnson was too frail to live on his own, so Bob Snoddon and his wife took him into their own home and looked after him until he went to be with the Lord.

Christmas 1945 we spent in Leominster with Joy, Daisy and Fred. Then it was off on deputation again, first round about England then in Scotland. While on Scottish deputation we stayed in W.E.C.'s Glasgow Headquarters. There we were able to have some lessons in French from a Christian lady who taught languages. We were back in Leominster in time for Joy's fifth birthday in March '46. It was about that time that we were able to introduce Fred and Daisy to Bill and Ena Pethybridge - the W.E.C. youth leaders. Fred was the Sunday School Superintendent at Leominster Baptist Church and he arranged for me to speak to the children one Sunday afternoon. There was a good response from that meeting among the young people - they became the nucleus of a Young Warrior group which Daisy and Fred started. As I said, their flat was above the Co-op stores but above that was a large disused store room. They cleared it out and turned it into a meeting place for Leominster young warriors. From then on Fred and Daisy became ever more deeply involved with W.E.C. At one particular conference in the Midlands the Lord

really spoke to them through Mr. Grubb about Christian steward-
ship and they dedicated their home to the Lord's work. Daisy and
Fred became real workers for W.E.C. at the home end.

Every summer Daisy and Fred would take the Leominster Young
Warriors to the W.E.C. camp at Kilcreggan in Scotland. At one of
these camps Thane Seager, the son of the head master of a primary
school in Leominster, was brought to faith in Christ. His parents
were members of Leominster Baptist Church. In 1963 I conducted
the wedding when Joy and Thane were married at that same Church.

Our time of furlough was drawing to a close. We spent Easter at
Gwystre Farm and Joy came with us. Gwystre Chapel had a flourishing Sunday School at that time - it was run by Iris and Dick Roberts
(Ivy's sister and youngest brother) several of the children were Joy's
cousins. They had asked me to lead a week's children's mission at
the Chapel during the school holiday. After the final meeting I felt
led to give an invitation to any boy or girl who wanted to receive the
Lord Jesus Christ as their Saviour to come out to the front. Almost
before I had finished giving the invitation Joy came running straight
down to the front of the Chapel. "What do you want, Joy?" I asked.
"I want to ask Jesus into my heart to be my Saviour", she replied.
Then some others came out and we prayed with them. Then we left
Gwystre to spend a few days with Ivy's eldest brother Hugh and his
family. They had a farm near Newtown in Montgomeryshire and a
little girl named Clarice who was a year younger than Joy. We were
telling them about the children's mission at Gwystre and Ivy had
Clarice sitting on her knee. We told how Joy had made a decision
for Christ, and then Ivy turned to Clarice and said - "Wouldn't you
like to do what Joy did and have the Lord Jesus Christ in your heart
to be your Saviour?" Clarice said, "Yes". So Ivy went and prayed
with her. Then Hugh came in and Clarice said to him quite sponta-
neously, "Daddy I'se a Christian as you'se a Christian". She was
just four years old - but Clarice has gone right on in the Faith, a
completely committed Christian with daughters of her own now.

By these means the Lord set His seal of blessing upon our first
furlough. Now it was time to return to the Congo - our passages
were booked for the end of April. Joy was now past her fifth birthday and had just started school. The evening before we had to leave

Leominster Daisy had put Joy to bed and then I went in to say 'good night' to her. Joy said to me, "Dad, do you think you are doing a good thing leaving your little girl?" I could only say, "Well, darling, it's the Lord's way for us and we have to go". She looked at me and said, "It's all right - as long as you're happy" - But we weren't happy - our hearts were breaking.

The next morning we took Joy off to school. Joy remembers that Ivy was carrying a bouquet of flowers for her teacher - she also remembers how happy and at peace she felt that morning. Ahead of us up the road she ran, dancing and hopping and skipping. Then she kissed us goodbye and ran into school. When we next saw Joy she was fourteen - her childhood had passed.

Thirteen years earlier Ivy had bade farewell to her parents on Leominster station and then she had cried and cried. Now we were leaving our child behind. The pain was indescribable - and yet there was along with the pain an inner peace. We were beginning to identify with the Apostle Paul when he wrote, "I am crucified with Christ; it is no longer I who live, but Christ lives in me; and the life which I now live in the flesh I live by faith - in the Son of God who loved me and gave Himself for me" (Galatians 2:20).

On our arrival back at W.E.C.'s London Headquarters we learned that our deeply respected field leader, Jack Harrison, had passed away unexpectedly while undergoing an operation - C. T. Studd's successor was just forty five years old. It was a stunning shock. His closest friend, Jack Scholes, had been appointed to succeed him as field leader.

During our furlough we had prayed much that the Lord would provide us with motor transport to get around the villages in place of our bicycles. Well, we found that the money had come in. So I searched for a suitable vehicle. Jack Kerrigan (the third of 'the three Jacks' who were at M.T.C. together) who was now with the Unevangelised Fields Mission in Congo, had a sturdy Commer van and recommended it. I inspected one in a garage in London and thought it ideal for our needs. So I paid for a Commer van in London and arranged to collect one from the Commer agent in Stanleyville. Then we went along to the Army and Navy Stores to be kitted out for our second term of overseas service.

Now I'll let Ivy finish off this chapter:

The War was long past when we travelled back to Africa - so we were able to take the normal route from Southampton through the Mediterranean and the Suez Canal to Mombasa, and then overland through Kenya and Uganda. Altogether it takes about a month to get out to the field that way. We had been so busy in London I hardly had time to think about it, but once that boat sailed away from Southampton the cost of it all just swept over me. I cried and cried. It had been bad enough leaving my dear parents. How small and broken and tearful my Mother had been. She could hardly lift her arm to wave to me and my Father just could not speak he was so choked with emotion - I shall never forget that last sight of them standing together on Leominster station. I did not know then that I would never see them again. Yet, now here I was, a mother leaving my own child behind. Such tremendous cost - only God can prepare you for it. For a long time we stood speechless by the rail as the ship sailed down Southampton Water, Bobby was holding my hand. Often on that voyage I would like to have a cry and Bobby would put his arms around me and say "Come on, darling what is it with you now?" Then I would talk about Joy and gently he would say, "You must be careful about crying, Ivy. You know what God has done for little Joy". I couldn't have had a better husband.

"Holiness unto the Lord" - that is the Scripture text inscribed inside my wedding ring. God had called us both to be missionaries - W.E.C. would never have accepted us otherwise. W.E.C. Crusaders never go out to the field just as missionary and wife but as two missionaries - both with a personal call from God to the work, and both ready to make any sacrifices for Christ - and missionary work does take hold of you. The same spiritual standard was demanded of our African students who went to Ibambi Bible School for training as evangelists. Their wives had to be at one with them - sharing their experience of the new birth, of Spirit-filled Christian living, ready to make sacrifices and live the life of a 'Gospel tramp'. A neighbouring Mission once reported in its magazine, "We held a week of meetings for evangelists and their wives. Unhappily, the latter are almost totally indifferent to the work of their husbands".

Such a situation could never have arisen among W.E.C. Crusaders or on a W.E.C. mission station.

When we arrived in Ibambi we were again reminded of the cost of Christian discipleship as we stood silently together at the freshly dug grave of Jack Harrison. It was alongside that of his predecessor, C.T. Studd.

At last we reached Malingwia. Jack and Olive (they had married while we were on furlough) were there to greet us. "Where's Lily?" we asked. "She's too ill to stay any longer. She's being evacuated", came the reply. The Mission truck that had brought us up to Malingwia took my sister Lily back to Ibambi. From there she was invalided home to Britain suffering from severe heart trouble. A few months later Lily died on the operating table at The Mildmay Christian Hospital in London. As in so many other ways my elder sister had gone on before.

•••

"And Jesus answered and said, 'Verily I say unto you. There is no one that hath left house, or brethren, or sisters, or father, or mother, or wife, or children, or lands, for My sake, and the gospel's, but he shall receive a hundredfold now in this time, houses, and brethren, and sisters, and mothers, and children, and lands with persecutions: and in the world to come eternal life."
Mark 10: 29 & 30.

Joy with husband Thane, and children Mark, Kevin, Corin and Vivian.

Chapter Ten

Consolidation

❖

WHAT A GOOD JOB OUR AFRICAN CHRISTIANS HAD DONE
AT MALINGWIA WHILE WE WERE ON FURLOUGH! WHEN
we left the forest had only just been cleared and building work
begun. Now the Station was fully functioning with church, school,
missionaries' houses, and dozens of little round African huts within
the compound. More important, under Jack and Olive and Lily's
guidance, there had been spiritual growth among the congregations.
It was a joy to be reunited with our African brethren and sisters,
especially those with whom we had deep bonds of affection because
they were our spiritual children. The Ababua loved their children.
We discovered that their hearts and homes were even more open to
us, for they understood what it had cost us to return to them without
our little girl.

Our former houseboy, Mattiasi, had just graduated from Ibambi
Bible School. When he had travelled around the villages with us he
had bombarded us with questions about the Scriptures - in that sense
he had always been in 'Bible School' but now he had matured into a
fine Christian. Shortly after his return Mattiasi married Twgwema -

a lovely young Christian woman who had been in the congregation since she was a girl. After their marriage Mattiasi was appointed pastor of the Malingwia Church - his long and fruitful ministry there has now (1994) lasted nearly fifty years. Even the pagans acknowledge that God has blessed Mattiasi. Altogether he and Twgwema have had eleven children (although two died in infancy) and their eldest son followed his father into Bible school and is now a pastor of the Zaire Protestant Church. Most pagans are polygamists yet, despite their many wives, they have only one or two children. They can see how God has blessed Mattiasi and Twgwema with nine.

Whenever we saw a place or object associated with Joy we longed to have her with us again. Yet Daisy was so kind and thoughtful. She took care that Joy kept in touch with us by helping her to write us a letter almost every week and by sending photos and pieces of her school work.

We had known that on our return to Malingwia there would be plenty of work to be done. All the buildings were temporary constructions made of the traditional materials - sticks, mud and grass - but the Africans wanted permanent buildings. So one of our first tasks was to get the brick-making machine. Ivy came along with me. We went in the mail van from Malingwia to Buta and then on to Stanleyville where we stayed with our friends Mr. and Mrs. Jenkinson of the U.F.M. There I collected the Commer van we had ordered in London and then the brick-making machine was loaded inside. On our return journey we stopped off half-way between Stanleyville and Buta to stay with our friends Mr. and Mrs. Jenkinson of the U.F.M. They had asked us to stay for the weekend and take the Sunday services on their station. We had such a happy time.

To operate the brick machine you needed four men - one to pull the lever, one to pour in the clay, one to take brick shapes away from the machine, and one to wheel them into the drying shed. That was the first thing we had to build the drying shed. Then we had to build a kiln - and we had to learn the skill of putting the dried bricks into the kiln. Then you had to cut piles and piles of firewood so that it was ready before burning begins. After the kiln has been fired it has to burn constantly day and night for a week. While I was home I had borrowed a book from the library about bricks and brick-making and read it up. How the people rejoiced when they saw those first beautifully baked bricks being carried up to the mission station - but it was all hard work. When we had made a large number of bricks we asked our African brethren what permanent brick building would they like to have constructed first of all. They said, "We want you to build your houses first". At that time we had two single ladies helping us - Muriel Harman (who delivered Joy) and Ellen Shaw. The Africans said "Build them a ladies' house". I was glad because their bungalow would be a small one with just two bedrooms and since I had never built a house before I would again be following the book. One of the most difficult jobs was putting on the aluminium roof. Our bungalow had to be much larger because we often had friends and visitors staying with us fellow W.E.C. crusaders, friends from the U.F.M. and the A.I.M. (Africa Inland Mission) whose field was beyond ours up on the border with the Sudan. They would stay with us when travelling through to Stanleyville. So the second bungalow we built had five bedrooms. By the time Robert was born in 1951 we had completed those two bungalows and made a start on the church.

During the first year of our second term Jack and Olive remained with us at Malingwia and then in 1947 they went on furlough. One of Jack's most important achievements was the development of the station's gardens. On our return we found that the gardens of all twenty African families were flourishing and that the station was self-sufficient in food. By the time Jack and Olive left Malingwia it was not only producing enough food for its residents but also enough to feed 150 school children - and selling vegetables to a nearby Portuguese coffee plantation. It was a tremendous encouragement to us that the African Christians on the station were not only ready to work hard at making bricks and on the construction of the station buildings and in their gardens, but they were also prepared to take responsibility for 100 school boys from Christian families who lived out in the villages, caring and providing for them. Before Jack left the committee of Africans which ran the Malingwia Church had organised education for the daughters of these Christian parents too. A number of widows from the villages had been converted. Several volunteered to come and live on the station and look after the school girls. So a 'village' of African huts was built for them in the compound - three or four girls to each widow's hut. In all there were places for 50 school girls. After Jack and Olive went on furlough Miss Dolores Myar from the United States came to help teach the girls.

As on our previous stations a typical day's programme at Malingwia would begin at 6 a.m. with parade and then Bible study. School would be from 7 to 8 a.m. - I would teach the workmen, Ivy their wives plus (with the help of monitors) the 100 or so boys, and one of the other lady missionaries would teach the girls. After an hour's break we would make bricks or work on a building from 9 a.m. until noon. Then in the afternoon the Africans would go and work in the gardens while the Europeans had a 'siesta'. In the evenings it would be 'camp fire ministry' or church meetings.

In 1946 Andre Yenga and Babandele joined our staff as "monitors" assisting Ivy with the boys' school. Andre came from the village of Pamir and was one of Bati's first converts. He was a very gentle, quiet man but an excellent school teacher and a gifted musician - he taught all the singing. Babandele came from a plantation near Koma. He was a strict disciplinarian and a fine school master.

At the end of that year (Christmas 1946) we held a week's conference at Malingwia for all the believers in our area. In they came from all the village churches as far away as Pamir in one direction or Bambise in the other. They had to walk - there was no other transport - they carried piles of food on their heads; it was a marvellous sight. There must have been five hundred Ababua believers at that conference. A decade earlier there hadn't been a single Christian in the region. How thankful to God we were for allowing us a share in such a thrilling and fruitful ministry.

Mattiasi was by then pastor of the Church at Malingwia. With his background as the child of a leper he naturally had a great concern for the many Ababua lepers in our region. While at Bible School in Ibambi Mattiasi had met Mrs. Moules and seen the work of the W.E.C. leprosarium at Nebobongo - he was particularly impressed by the village for 'clean' children. These children had been taken from their leprous mothers when they were born because leprosy is only contagious not hereditary. Under his influence the Conference decided to put in a request to W.E.C. to build a leprosarium like Nebobongo at Malingwia.

Many were concerned for their friends who had leprosy. They said, "If you can get permission from the Government we are willing to clear the forest and build little huts for those who have leprosy so that they can be treated". So we wrote on behalf of the Conference to our field leader, Jack Scholes. Jack and his field committee were in sympathy with the project. Then I wrote to the Belgian official who had been so helpful in getting us the concession at Malingwia. Now, the wonderful thing is that that official had been promoted and posted to Stanleyville as a full commissar. He replied immediately to my letter expressing his pleasure that the Africans had initiated the proposal, that they had caught the vision of helping their own people. He said that he was going to send up some of his officials to see what was required - and they came. They obtained permission from the Paramount Chief and then measured out a large concession for us - and the people were just thrilled to see the Lord opening-up the way for their leprosarium through these officials.

There was a young couple working at Nebobongo with Mrs. Moules (Percy Moules had died of typhoid fever in October 1944 less than four years after they were married) - this couple were Arthur and Irene Scott. Irene was a trained nurse and they had three young daughters (one of them - Barbara - is now in her third term as a W.E.C. missionary in Senegal). When they heard about our leprosy project they volunteered to come and start the work at Malingwia. This took place at about the same time that Edith Moules founded a new branch of W.E.C. called "The Leprosy and Medical Crusade" (1947).

The following year Dudu and Edidi came to us and said that they wanted to go to the Ibambi Bible School. Ever since we went on furlough in 1944 they had been teaching their wives - especially Dudu's wife who hadn't been able to read or write when we left. Dudu said that both wives were now able to pass the elementary education test required for entry into Bible School. Well, that rejoiced our hearts and we put their request before their church committee at Sombo.

The committee were happy to recommend and support Dudu and Edidi through Bible school. They said, "We're going to miss Dudu and Edidi because they are so dedicated to God's work, but its good to know that we will have two full-time evangelists". So Dudu and Edidi and their wives went off to Ibambi where they had to learn Kingwana before they could begin their courses of study. Two years later they returned as fully trained evangelists. The Church committee sent Dudu and his wife to be full-time pastor / evangelist to the growing church at Komo. Bati requested that Edidi should come to Pamir and help him. There were so many opportunities in the surrounding villages and along the railway line, but as a self-supporting catechist Bati didn't have the time. So Edidi and his wife were sent to Pamir as evangelists to work alongside Bati - and there was a tremendous response in that area to their ministry.

Now that we had the van we could travel to more distant villages than we had been able to reach on our cycles. Dudu, working up among the plantation people at Komo, became interested in the neighbouring Bizande tribe whose territory lay to the north of the Bomokandi River. Mattiasi also had a great concern for this tribe. Was it, perhaps, because the Bizande had traditionally been enemies of the Ababua? Often I would drive up to Komo and then cross the river by pontoon to preach in the villages of the Bizande. The A.I.M. had missionaries working among the Bizande people but their stations were much further east towards the Sudanese border. Two couples became good friends of ours. Mr. and Mrs. Dix had established a station at Banda near the Uele River and later they had been joined by Dr. and Mrs. Brown who began a medical work there. They would stay overnight with us at Malingwia when they were travelling down to Buta or Stanleyville to get supplies.

In 1951 Ivy was expecting Robert and we knew we would have to go to a place where there was a doctor and a nurse for her confinement. When Dr. Brown knew that Ivy was pregnant he invited us to come up to Banda when the time came. Whenever he was passing through Malingwia he would check that everything was progressing normally. On one occasion he actually sent his young assistant to see if Ivy was keeping well. In July we travelled up to Banda. Everything had been prepared for us; what a comfort it was to be in the care of a Christian doctor. How the Lord does provide for his servants!

The delivery went "super-well" and Robert was born on 21st July 1951 - ten years after Joy. After Joy had been born at Poko we had taken her back to the villages to live in African huts and share our 'gypsy life', but now we brought our second child back to Malingwia to live in a brick bungalow. Robert grew up on the mission station.

•••

"Except the LORD build the house, they labour in vain
that build it; Except the LORD keep the city, the watchman
waketh but in vain."
Psalm 127: 1

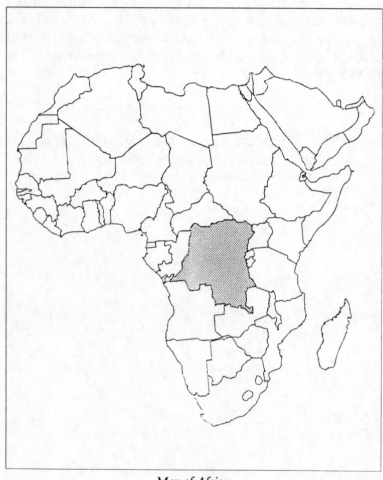

Map of Africa.
Shaded area is the Congo (now Zaire).

Chapter Eleven

Revival at Malingwia[*]

— ❖ —

THE CHURCH COMMITTEE AT MALINGWIA CAME TO US ONE DAY WITH A REQUEST, "COULDN'T WE HAVE A doctor at the Leprosarium here? Mr. & Mrs. Scott are doing a fine job, and Mrs. Scott is a wonderful nurse but a lot of the people here have illnesses that need treatment by a doctor" - that would have been in the year before Robert was born. We replied, "Well there is no harm in writing and asking because the Scripture says "Ask and ye shall receive..." When they said, "'We would like to write a letter to Mr. Grubb". (They knew Mr. Grubb because he had come out to the Congo and visited the station and they knew that he spoke Bangala and had translated much of the Scriptures into their language). So the Africans wrote to Mr. Grubb in Bangala and I posted their letter to our London headquarters in Upper Norwood. The very day that this letter was received a young doctor called in and spoke to Mr. Grubb. He said that he felt called to do leprosy work in the Congo. Mr. Grubb showed him the letter written in Bangala which he had received that very morning. It was a thrilling confirmation for Dr. John Harris. What wonderful timing! Our God is the One who works to time!

[*]   Further information on the Congo Revival of the early 1950s can be found in "This is That" published by the Christian Literature Crusade in 1954.

By the time John Harris arrived on the field Robert was nearing his second birthday and Mr. & Mrs. Scott had gone home on furlough. John was sent straight up to Malingwia to begin language study. It was a Saturday in June or July 1953 when the mission truck was driven into the station bearing John Harris and his luggage - accompanying him were Jack Scholes and Mary Harrison (the widow of Jack Harrison). Almost as soon as the truck stopped the driver jumped out and ran up to us saying "We've come with good news. God is doing a mighty work among my people in Ibambi and down at Wamba. God has been convicting us that we have to deal with the ashes of sin in our lives if God's fire is to be kept burning brightly." It was by means of this truck driver that God brought revival to Malingwia.

We had heard about a visitation of the Holy Spirit upon other parts of the field through the letters of our fellow missionaries. Together with the Ababua believers we longed to share in that blessing and had been waiting prayerfully and expectantly for several months. So we were prepared for the revival when it came the weekend that John Harris arrived.

The W.E.C. field now extended about 400 miles from east to west and 450 miles north to south. The revival had begun the previous February during a local workers conference at Lubutu which was our most southern station - the far end of the field from us. Messages had been given on the Person and work of the Holy Spirit and there had arisen a general desire for God to meet with them. At an evening prayer meeting the African evangelists and their wives were suddenly overcome by a violent shaking; weeping and confession of sin followed - the meeting went on for hours. After the missionaries had finally got to bed one of them was awakened by his house boy who was shaking under conviction and wanted to confess to stealing from the house.

The blessing continued for weeks and spread to village churches in the district. Then two of our missionaries from the station at Opienge, together with some African believers from the Bomili section of the Ituri forest, visited Lubutu. They were the means of the revival spreading northwards across the Lindi River to Bomili and the Mabari tribe. From there it spread to Ibambi and then almost immediately on to our area in the deep forest - God's means being the visit of an African evangelist and his wife from Lubutu.

But back to that first memorable weekend: with tears in his eyes, the truck driver from Ibambi said to me, "My sin has been doing God's work with a moan and a groan. I knew that I could earn more money as a truck driver than the Mission paid me and I was coveteous of a better-paid job". He was just full of it. He said, "If I don't confess and make things right God will 'spew me out of His mouth' as it says in the Book of Revelation." I could see that God had done a work in Him. Before when he drove into the station he would shout "Call your men to unload the truck" and go and sit in the shade - but now he was happily and whole heartedly unloading the baggage of our new young doctor.

That Saturday evening the truck driver told us about the spread of the revival to Ibambi. Muriel Harman and Ellen Shaw had taken over from the Scotts at the leprosarium and Dolores Myar were still working with us. So with Jack Scholes and Mary Harrison there were seven of us missionaries listening to his story. John Harris was also sitting there but he didn't yet speak a word of Bangala so he couldn't understand what was going on. Then the truck driver went down to the village in the compound and told it all over again to the Africans.

He was aglow - you could see the revival in his face - he was so full of it. Soon there was the sound of singing from the African's huts - singing that went on late into the night. You see, we had held a monthly day of prayer for revival and everyone on the station was full of expectancy, wondering how the revival would come to us.

The next day I asked the driver to speak at our Sunday morning service and tell the packed congregation about the happenings in Lubutu, Opienge, Wamba, Ibambi and all over our field. He spoke for a long time. I was sitting on the platform with him and could see the effect his words were having on our people. There was real conviction in that meeting, a hundred school boys and fifty school girls just sat there listening - there was no fidgeting. Husbands and wives with their babies sat quietly. At the end of the service I said, "Now go and prepare yourselves for the afternoon meeting" - and they did - they went and gave themselves over to prayer.

Shortly before the time of the service to our amazement a tropical storm swept in - the wind was lashing the rain along in great horizontal gusts. Our churches are built with half-open sides to allow air to circulate so in a storm the rain would lash right through the building. We turned to John Harris and Muriel Harman and said, "That's it! There'll be no meeting this afternoon". Usually rapid rhythmic drum beats call the people to worship but there was no sound from the drums. Then above the howling storm we heard singing - all the Africans were in the church soaked by the gusts of driving rain, yet singing at the tops of their voices. So we thought that we had better go too. We put on our macks and made our way through the storm to the church feeling rather ashamed to be the last to arrive. Then the truck driver started again telling how God was convicting Christians of their spiritual coldness, that they cannot be cold or lukewarm because of the ashes of sin, that unless they were "burning hot" God would "spew them out of His mouth". After speaking a long time he turned to me and asked me to close the meeting in prayer. Then to my amazement everyone stood up - children, teenagers, adults - it was as if they all knew what to do - yet no one had said a word. Then I heard weeping. I looked up and saw that the school boys were weeping, I looked over to the girl's side and they were weeping, I looked over their heads to the adults and many of them were weeping and broken-up under real conviction.

Suddenly down the aisle and out in front of the whole church ran Kebo. She lifted up her arms and cried out - "I'm a thief, I'm a thief". Then she fell prostrate weeping and weeping, her tiny baby still on her back. Then some of the other women ran forward, lifted her up and put their arms around her - and they began weeping. These older women said "We should have helped Kebo. We should have cared for her. We shouldn't have told tales about her. We should have given her food".

You see, for many months these women had been coming to me making complaints about Kebo - they accused her of stealing food from their gardens. When Kebo was brought to us she would start crying and refused to admit that she was taking anything. She said that they were just telling lies about her. Kebo was the wife of our house boy, Nembobo. She was only a young girl and expecting their first child, and she probably didn't have the energy to work hard in the garden like the other women.

After Kebo had confessed another woman came crawling on her hands and knees to the front followed by her husband. They confessed that they had been unhappy living together and were always quarrelling. Then the crowd around Kebo began to sing in Bangala the chorus "rolled away, rolled away, and the burden of my heart rolled away". Their faces were beaming with the joy of the Lord. Then the whole congregation took up the singing, and they sang and sang that chorus until it was nearly dark. We thought they would never stop. Then we all went home full and overflowing with joy - God had broken through.

Next morning (Monday) the truck driver had to return to Ibambi. We tried to return to the normal work-day routine but somehow we couldn't settle to it. So we called the congregation together after school had finished. However there was such a deadness in the meeting. One lad tried to urge them on but you cannot work up such things - the Holy Spirit brings down conviction - so we restrained him. We divided the congregation up into groups - boys, girls, wives, workmen - and set them to seek the Lord in prayer. Tremendous intercession poured forth all over the church yet, strangely, I couldn't feel a burden of prayer for the school boys. So I pleaded with them to open their hearts and yield to the Lord. I couldn't say any more. I just broke down and wept and wept. Then the little boys broke down; at first the older ones continued to resist, then they too broke. Many confessed to petty thieving especially to shop lifting when they went into the neighbouring town of Titule. We said, "You must take everything back". Later we started a Boys' Brigade company for them.

That weekend our house boy, Nembobo, confessed that he had resented the visits of our friends the missionaries of the A.I.M. when they were travelling through Malingwia because of the extra work they made. Perhaps his confession was prompted by his wife's experience - Kebo was a new woman. On another occasion Andre Yenga opened his heart to us confessing his lack of consideration for his wife. For a long time we had been worried about Manzegie. We couldn't understand why she seemed so unhappy - she was a good mother with a lovely little family but there was no joy.   Ivy talked with her several times but we could never break through this heaviness of spirit. Now they came to us together and Andre said, "The Lord has convicted me. It's not that I'm doing God's work 'with a moan and a groan'. I am doing God's work with all my heart but I have been neglecting my wife. I have not been considerate towards Manzegie. I have left her to bear the burden of the children alone". It was true Manzegie did have to work so very hard for, not only did they have five small children of their own, but they took their share of responsibility for the school boys. All the Christian families living on the station took in two or three boys from the villages and cared for them - a hundred school boys were divided up among the people. It was a lot of extra work especially for the women. They had to fetch firewood from the forest, plantains from their gardens, water from the well - all on their heads. So God convicted Andre. He turned to Manzegie and knelt before her. Weeping he confessed to her that he hadn't been helping her as he should and asked her forgiveness. What a change came over Manzegie - she came right through to joy and assurance in the Lord - all the resentment was gone. Manzegie yielded right over to the Lord - all the women were blessed through her experience.

A fortnight later we had our second womens' conference. In 1952 a hundred women had attended, this year over two hundred came to Malingwia. From the outset the Holy Spirit was poured upon those meetings. It was simply wonderful - like something out of the Wesley or Whitfield journals. There was such conviction of sin. Ivy reported at the time: "There were no messages, the women were just smitten down to the ground on all sides, falling, writhing in terrible agony. They seemed to see all their life pass before them like a cinema; they truly saw hell and feared".

During the Conference God particularly spoke to these Christian women about the wearing of jewellery. Ndaka, the wife of Mbo another house boy, was particularly fond of decorating her body and hair. One day she went to a nearby garden to seek the Lord in prayer wearing her jewellery. Almost immediately she was given a vision. Her ears and ear-rings grew so large and became so heavy that she was imprisoned by them. Then someone clothed in white stood

beside her and told her to open the Bible at 1 Timothy 2:9 - 15 and at
II Peter 1: 12 & 13. Just then her husband arrived on the scene. At
first she was quite unaware of his presence. When he asked her
what was wrong Ndaka asked him to fetch his Bible and read those
passages of Scripture to her because she couldn't read. Off came
her jewellery. Later when Ndaka recounted her vision to the women
gathered at the Conference God dealt with all of them. One by one
they took off their ear-rings, beads, and bangles and brought them
out to the front and put them into a hat. Afterwards it was thrown
into a deep pit.

We were particularly burdened that husbands and wives should
come through together to a shared experience of God's blessing because the average African couple had little of love and home-life as
we know it. The fruits of that God-given concern were seen in Thursday's meetings. Wives and husbands stood on the platform: weeping together with arms around each other. Several testified openly
to the great joy and love that God had given. One woman standing
with her husband said, "Now I love my husband like a child". The
African women had a great love for their children - but love for their
husbands was much less common. From the platform we looked out
upon a sea of shining faces.

When the evangelists and catechists from the villages were about
to return home we gathered for a final early morning meeting. However that meeting lasted from 6.30 until 10.30 a.m. Couples from
Malingwia - husbands and wives together came to the front of the
church testifying to a clear call from God to go to this unreached
area or that needy place. Then young couples, mostly our former
school children recently married with the beginnings of families,
came out saying that God had called them to go to Ibambi Bible
School.

Another result of the Conference was the womens' mission to
Korosa. Often we had referred to Korosa as "the cement area" because of its spiritual hardness. It was the only unresponsive district
in our whole area. One day twelve of the station women - including
Manzegie, Kabo and Mbo - came to us and said "God has put on
our hearts to go and visit that place which you call 'the cement area'".
By the 1950s these women were benefiting from the proceeds from

the sale of cotton as much as their husbands, many had their own sewing machines and bicycles. They said, "We have got permission from our husbands. They are willing to take over and look after the children for a week. It will do them good". "So we're off". Away they went cycling down through Titule and Bambili to Korosa where they stayed about a week.

Afterwards, Jim Grainger acting field leader, visited Korosa - he estimated that over four thousand people had been converted. God had broken the hard cement! Everywhere people were seeking God. Near Korosa there was a coffee plantation owned by a Dutch company and a young Dutch couple managed it. They spoke perfect English and whenever I was visiting the little plantation church they always invited me to have a meal with them. They were a friendly but worldly couple. The wife was a chain smoker, a cigarette was always hanging from her mouth. She would say to me, "You are only wasting your time with these people". One weekend during the revival I drove out to the plantation. During the meal she remarked, "Things are happening here. The Africans are bringing back things they have stolen. Can I come to your church tomorrow morning?" I was staggered.

Sure enough there they both were on Sunday morning sitting on the back bench in our tiny plantation church - sitting among their own African workmen. So I said to the new believers, "We want you to give your testimonies". One by one they stood up came to the front and simply told what the Lord had done for them. From the platform I could see that the Dutch lady had started to cry. Babandele preached that morning and she wept all through his message. After the service she came to me and said, "Mr. Milliken can I come and stay on your station with Mrs. Milliken for a few days?" I replied "Sure. Come along". So when I returned to Malingwia on Monday morning she came with me. Naturally Ivy was surprised to see her and even more so when she said, "I want to be with you because I feel I must do something". We warned her that since the revival there were now Christian meetings every night. She asked "Can I come with you?" One night after a meeting at which Dudu had preached she turned to him and confessed "I'm a slave to smoking". Dudu said, "Give me your cigarettes. Get the packets out of your handbag". They prayed together then Dudu said, "Light a fire". They threw her packets of cigarettes on to the fire and the African believers sang. Do you know that woman was completely delivered! She never smoked another cigarette after that night. Even better, she and her husband were both converted soon after. It was Europeans as well as Africans who were blessed by the revival.

For the remainder of their tour of duty they were very generous to our African believers on their plantation. Then the time came for their furlough. They came to stay with us at Malingwia before they left for Holland. We prayed with them and introduced them to regular Bible reading. On their way home by boat they dined at the captain's table. Do you know they led the German captain of that liner to the Lord!

They wrote to us from Holland saying, "God has used us to convert the ship's captain" - and while they were at home God used them to be a blessing to their relatives. When they returned to the Congo their company sent them to manage a plantation near Paulis. Our station at Nala was nearby and our workers were building a brick church in the town of Paulis itself. The husband was very artistic and a skilled sign writer. So when the church was finished he decorated the interior walls with texts from Scripture. Those two Dutch people were soundly converted and they became just like missionaries working among their fellow Europeans in Paulis.

Perhaps the greatest change brought by the revival was in the atmosphere of our station - and that has lasted. . When the revival started the school children contacted their parents back in the villages urging them to come and experience it for themselves. When they arrived at the station they exclaimed, "Malingwia has changed - there's a different spirit here. Now when we come we are welcomed with open arms. Before everybody was busy, now they have time to care for us". Even the pagan people living around recognise the change. They said, "Everything's different at Malingwia".

Yes everything was different. There was a spirit of joy and happiness. This was especially noticeable in the prayer meetings. Usually in these meetings individuals will lead in prayer one after another often with gaps in between, but the revival brought a great burden in prayer. Everybody prayed - yet there wasn't any chaos or disorder - they all prayed together about a specific matter until the burden lifted then someone would finish it off. A few years ago (1989) Dr. Helen Roseveare revisited our former stations in the Congo. Afterwards she wrote telling us about her trip and she reported, "There's a marvellous spirit at Malingwia. Among the churches I visited it is the closest to the old revival spirit."

•••

"Bring ye all tithes into the storehouse, that there may be meat in mine house, and prove me now herewith, saith the LORD of hosts, if I will not open for you the windows of heaven, and pour you out a blessing, that there shall not be room enough to receive it."
Malachi 3:10

Chapter Twelve

Second Furlough

---------------------- ❖ ----------------------

THINGS WERE HAPPENING ALL THE TIME DURING THE REVIVAL. ROBERT WAS ABOUT TWO WHEN IT STARTED. He played with the little children on the station as he learned to speak and so his first language was Bangala. Ivy would speak to him in English and he understood what she was saying but he always replied in Bangala. Each Sunday morning before the service Ivy would have a little service with about fifty of these tiny tots under five on our verandah with a couple of the older school girls to help her. One very busy Sunday morning Ivy suddenly exclaimed, "Oh, I've forgotten all about the children." Her assistants were away that morning. She hurried back to our bungalow imagining what disasters could have occurred. When she got there nobody was running around, all these tiny children were sitting quietly in a circle. A young girl about ten years old named Maria had taken charge - and who was sitting in the centre of the circle like a little mouse? Robert! Maria was saying to him:

We must not be disobedient. I used to be rebellious and disobedient when my mother wanted me to look after the twins. If we want to please God we must obey our parents. Now, Robert, you are a naughty boy and you have got to stop being naughty. When your mother comes out of school she calls 'Robert where are you?' Instead of going to your mother you run away and hide and then she asks "Where's Robert? Where's Robert?" and you are hiding. You're a naughty boy". By this time Robert was crying. Then he saw his Mum standing listening. Up he got and ran to her crying in Bangala: "I'm not a bad boy, I'm not a bad boy am I Mummy?"

Well, Ivy wasn't sure how to reply as she took him in her arms - but that was the sort of way the Holy Spirit was working in Malingwia at that time.

Robert's spiritual experience was different from Joy's although both were converted by the time they were five. Robert's was more gradual. He was very fond of a dear old African Christian man named Kalibati. When Robert was about three Kalibati died. Like all the children on the station Robert was at the burial service and he began to cry and cry. We said, "Robert, don't cry. Kalibati is in heaven now". "No he's not," sobbed Robert, "because he's in that box". Afterwards we tried to explain very simply to him that the bodies of Christian believers are temples of the Holy Spirit and that our spirits go to be with Jesus in heaven. He seemed to understand.

Now that Robert was no longer a baby Ivy used to go with me when I went out preaching in the forest villages. Many of them couldn't be reached in our van so we still had to use bicycles. I built a sort of one-wheeled sedan chair for Ivy to ride in with Robert from the back end of an old bike - the Africans called it a "push push". Once during the school holidays we used it for a month riding around the villages. However, the van did allow us to travel to the more distant parts of our area. On a Friday night I would gather together the African believers and tell them that we would be going on an evangelistic trip the next day to a particular area and ask for volunteers to go with me. Before the revival they would often be reluctant to go saying (quite correctly) that they had been working hard all week in the cotton fields, in their gardens and on the station buildings - and Saturday was their hunting day. It meant something for them to give up their weekend. Yet when the revival came God convicted them about their unwillingness to spend the weekend away.

So nearly every Saturday I would crowd as many as I could into the van and we would be off to some distant group of villages. Then I would drop them off in pairs in different villages along the way and pick them up again on the way home the following evening.

Every aspect of the work was now vibrant and developing. We built a church and an orphanage and home for the lepers' children at the leprosarium and introduced an irrigation project which gave improved crop yields in gardens and fields. Dr. John Harris performed a successful operation to remove an eye growth from a local Portuguese coffee plantation owner in the leprosarium hospital. As an expression of thanks he gave us an old truck which we cannibalised. Its front wheels, steering and suspension proved particularly useful - I modified them, and built John's first adjustable operating table!

These years of our second term in the Congo were some of the happiest of our entire ministry. What a blessing it was seeing the work build up, experiencing the revival, and sending off some of our young couples to Ibambi Bible School. It was during 1953/4 that Bob and Bess Butters (American supporters of W.E.C.) visited us on the field. They were very interested in medical work - they had a daughter who was training to be a doctor - and they had taken a great interest in the development of the leprosarium. Bob and Bess brought a cine camera with them and took film of the work at Ibambi and Malingwia - that film is now a valuable historical record of African missions as they used to be.

We had been out on the field nearly nine years and the Mission said that it was time for us to go on furlough. They sent an older couple - Mr. & Mrs. English to replace us . Once they had settled in we set off on the first stage of our journey back to England. Just before we left Malingwia Ivy presented her devoted assistant teacher, Andre Yenga, with her concertina. He was a fine musician and would make good use of it.

First of all we travelled down to Nala where Jack and Olive were still in charge of the station. It was during this period that they were building the church in Paulis. Jack had asked me to come and help them put the aluminium roof on the building which was always a difficult job. When it was done we went down to Ibambi. Robert was so excited. We had shown him photographs of Joy and now soon he would be seeing his sister for the first time. Jack Scholes drove us to the Uganda border in the mission truck. There we stayed with an American couple on the A.I.M. mission station at Kasenyi before crossing Lake Albert into Uganda. Bangala was the trade language of that district and so our friends knew Bangala. On our arrival the American lady turned to Ivy and asked "What can I get Robert to drink?" Robert (who was now four) spoke up for himself in Bangala " I drink goats milk". Amazed, the lady asked "What did you say?" So Robert repeated his request in Bangala. How everyone laughed. Rather apologetically our friend then answered "I am sorry, Robert, we don't have goats here. We only have cows milk". You see, we didn't have cows at Malingwia - they couldn't survive there because of the tsetse fly.

How different that second journey home was from the first in 1944. The steamer takes nearly a day to cross Lake Albert and then we had a lovely ride through Uganda and Kenya down to Mombassa. There we boarded the liner and enjoyed a three week holiday/voyage to England. On the boat there were quite a number of children and gradually Robert came to realise that he had to speak in English if he wanted to communicate with them. There was one girl on the boat about the same age as Joy and she had her hair in plaits too. One day Robert said "Mummy, is our Joy like that girl over there?" We said that she was like her - so that helped him. His biggest difficulty was in adjusting to British food - he was used to Congolese food and wanted an African menu!

After we passed through the Suez Canal the ship put in at Alexandria. There we made several trips out into the Mediterranean in glass bottomed boats to see marvellously coloured fish swimming beneath us. It was a wonderful sight. Our ship docked at Tilbury one September day in 1955. This time everyone knew when we were arriving. We went up to London and then straight on to Leominster. Fred and Daisy were at the station to meet us but Joy had just gone back to the Grammar school after the summer holiday and was starting her G.C.E. courses. What a lovely reunion we had together when she came in from school! How pleased Robert was to meet his sister at last! It had been eight years since we last saw Joy. She was six when we left for Congo; she was now fourteen.

As it happened one evening in Leominster coincided with the weekly meeting of the Young Warriors in the room above the flat. Of course we joined them. During the meeting Joy gave her testimony telling the group how she had received the Lord Jesus Christ as her Saviour in Gwystre Chapel when she was a little girl. About midnight we were woken up by the sound of muffled sobbing coming from Robert's little bed which was beside ours. We put on the light and asked Robert what was wrong:

"Are you feeling ill?" we asked.

"I'm all right", he replied. "But, I'd thought to have the Lord Jesus in my heart as my Saviour and Joy told us tonight that she had taken the Lord Jesus into her heart to be her Saviour. There's only one Jesus - so what can I do? I'll have to go to hell."

And then he burst out crying so pitifully. Ivy took him in her arms as I said:

"Listen, Robert. That's true. There is only one Jesus - there's God the Father, God the Son (Jesus) and God the Holy Spirit. But when Jesus comes into the heart it is by the Holy Spirit. So Joy can have Jesus in her heart, Dad has Jesus and I have Jesus - and you can have Jesus. But before Jesus will come into your heart you must pray the sinners' prayer, 'Lord be merciful to me, a sinner'. Now when Maria spoke to you in Malingwia you said you were not a sinner. If you want Jesus to come into your heart you must know that you are a sinner and that you need Him to be your Saviour from sin".

"Oh yes," he said. "I am a sinner. I went with Aunty Daisy to her school and took away that little car." He also mentioned other naughty things he had done. Then I said:

"Now you've told Jesus that you are a sinner and you want him to be your Saviour. So ask Him." Then he prayed:

"Come into my heart Lord Jesus. Come in today. Come in to stay. Come into my heart, Lord Jesus".

The transaction had been completed and little Robert knew it. He went back to bed and slept peacefully until morning.

The Africans had prayed that the spirit of revival would follow Robert to England, until he became broken, and convicted of sin. Their prayer was answered.

We spent the rest of the year 1955 in Leominster. During that time we received an invitation from Bob and Bess Butters to visit them in America. They offered to arrange a tour of American churches and Bible colleges where we could give them an eye witness account of the Congo revival. The Mission allowed us to accept their offer, and so Bob and Bess organised a six-month itinerary which would take us right across the U.S.A. The question to be faced first though was whether to take Robert or leave him in Britain. Ivy's sisters Violet and Iris were willing enough to have Robert stay with them but he didn't settle in the way Joy had. There was no clear word from the Lord and we had no peace about it. Since our last furlough W.E.C. had established a home for their missionaries' children at Arbroath in Scotland which was run by our old Congo associates, Charlie & Lily Searle. So we took Robert up to Arbroath to see how he would get on at the home - it would prepare him for the time when we would return to the Congo field. Ivy's family, however, were not happy that Robert - who was not yet five should be so far away from them up in Scotland, but we felt it was the right place for him, so we left him there.

Our American trip lasted longer than six months. Everywhere we went people listened enthralled as we recounted our experiences of the Lord's reviving work in the Congo. While we were speaking to the students and staff of one particular Bible college a young student named Bill McChesney heard the Lord's call to service in the Congo and responded. Four years later he arrived at Wamba to begin language study. In 1961 he came up to Malingwia. When we had last met back in 1956 he had been at Bible college in America - now here he was serving his first term on the field. Three years later Bill was captured by the Simba rebels and imprisoned at Wamba. When news came through that Stanleyville had been recaptured by the United Nations forces the rebels' anger erupted. The full fury of their hatred was reserved for the Belgians and Americans. Bill was clubbed and tortured, and then, at the end of December 1964 was ordered out of the prison. His friend and fellow missionary Jim

Rodgers had to support him in his arms - they were both shot dead, both martyred in their prime of life.

After we returned from America the Mission sent us on an extended deputation tour of Ireland where we again described our experiences of the revival. This time we took Robert with us. My Father who was now getting on in years was able to meet his grandson. We spent some weeks in Belfast and I went along regularly to The Welcome Mission to help with the work. Before we returned to England we were approached by the trustees and asked to consider taking on the pastorate of the Mission - but our call was still to W.E.C. and the Congo.

In the course of our travels around Britain the Mission sent us down to speak at Swansea Bible College. There we discovered that Rees Howells had not only founded a Bible School but also Emmanuel Grammar School - a boarding school for missionaries' children. We spoke to the lady in charge of the younger boys and she suggested that we bring Robert to see the school. Of course Swansea suited Ivy's family very well since most of them were still living in central Wales. Ivy's younger brother Joseph and his wife Eileen had a sheep farm at Norton near Presteign in Radnorshire. They said that Robert could go and stay with them during the school holidays and bring with him any school friends he chose. Robert grew to love Black Patch Farm - he lived for the school holidays and would have liked nothing better than to be a farmer himself. Not only did Robert's Uncle Joe look after him during the school holidays, he also paid all his school fees and expenses at Emmanuel. Joseph and Eileen attended Ackhill Baptist Church near Presteign and there (in the river) Robert was baptised when he was 15.

Anyway, to get back to 1958 when he was seven. We took Robert down to Swansea and he liked the School, perhaps because there were sixty children there including several boys his own age and they were all in the same situation - being all the children of missionaries. Mr. Warren was in charge of the boys' dormitory and Robert seemed to get on well with him. The Mission allowed us to remain an extra year in Britain to ensure that Robert had settled in at Swansea but then - after his eighth birthday - it was time to us to return for our third term of service.

By this time Joy was eighteen, had left school and was about to go to teacher training college. Joy and Robert grew up separately, seeing each other several times a year. I had been asked to go and speak at Swansea Bible College for our final weekend. Joy came to Leominster Station with us and said goodbye, and then we took the train down to Swansea. We spent the time with Robert until crowds of people started arriving for the evening service and I knew I had to go. Then Mr. Warren came along and told us that it was time for the boys to go to bed.

So I kissed Robert goodbye and went across to the College. After I left, Robert turned to Ivy and said, "Dad's gone. There's only you left now, Mum". Ivy couldn't hold back her tears any longer. Mr. Warren was very kind. He said he would come down to Swansea Station and tell us how Robert had reacted to our leaving. The next morning he was there at the Station and told us that Robert had slept soundly through the night and gone off to school without any complaint or fuss. Every child is different and the Lord dealt with Robert in a different way to Joy. Robert took longer to settle but it's wonderful how the Lord provides. Gradually it became obvious that the Lord had provided a place for him in Swansea and with his Uncle Joe at Black Patch Farm.

When we left Leominster Joy gave us a copy of "Daily Light". Inside the cover she wrote "To Daddy and Mummy on their return to the Congo" and she gave us three Scripture promises, Luke 18 29 & 30 was among them. That little book is very precious to us. We have used it every day since Joy gave it in 1959. It's getting a bit worn now.

•••

"Behold children are a heritage from the LORD: the fruit of the womb is His reward."
Psalm 127: 3

Chapter Thirteen

Unexpected Exit

❖

OUR VOYAGE TO MOMBASA IN THAT SUMMER OF 1959 (AND SUBSEQUENT JOURNEY BACK WESTWARDS through Kenya and Uganda) was quite unremarkable - just like that of thousands of other British expatriates serving in East Africa during the post-war years. How ignorant we were of those "winds of change" that were about to blow away settled systems of government and patterns of life.

We returned to Malingwia and found evidences of the revival everywhere. The station was thriving - its buildings a hive of activity - the new brick church well on the way to completion. Mr. and Mrs English were in control of the station assisted by a young Australian, Pat Holdaway. Malingwia didn't need us. So after a few weeks the field committee sent us down to Lubutu.

Lubutu is a large town about three hundred miles south of Ibambi. The station just outside the town had been established in 1936 by Jim and Ida Grainger. By 1959 it had a brick church but no school. The young couple serving there, David and Margaret Waller, were anxious to begin a school. David was a teacher and Margaret a nurse

- but they were only in their first term and the senior couple, Cyril and Joy Taylor, were home in New Zealand on furlough. Jim Grainger our acting field leader naturally took a close interest in the work there. So we were asked to stay in Lubutu until the Taylors returned from furlough. We were there for nearly a year and what a happy time that was! David asked Bobby to build him a school - he had all the bricks ready and waiting - so Bobby built him a school. What with teaching and preaching (in Kingwana again) we were kept very busy.

The field council was exploring the possibility of setting up another Bible school in the southern part of the Mission's territory. Lowa situated on the Western bank of the great River Congo was the town they had in mind. Bobby went down to survey the proposed site but found the ground totally unsuitable. When he reported back to the field council he suggested that the Bible school be established in Lubutu. Later, when we were back in England, we learned that the Taylors had started building at Molita - even further to the south - but the work was barely begun when the Simba Rebellion broke out.

Everything was normal and peaceful when we drove up to Ibambi for the 1960 Ibambi Conference. Great political events were taking place far off to the West in Léopoldville but here in North-East Congo all was as usual, and anyway we were too busy to give the politicians a second thought. Nevertheless the Conference agenda was to be dominated by the implications of political developments ahead.

During our extended furlough we often heard the name Patrice Lumumba and gathered that nationalism was spreading throughout the Congo. Just before our return there had been rioting in Léopoldville in which Europeans had been attacked and their property destroyed. As we were arriving for our third term Lumumba was demanding immediate independence and King Baudoin was promising it for the following year. The Belgian administration was making little effort to train Congolese replacements. Many politically-minded Africans thought independence and freedom from colonial rule would mean the right to dispossess the Europeans - but we knew nothing of this as we drove towards Ibambi.

Every station and aspect of the Mission's work was represented at the Conference - Mattiasi was Malingwia's representative. The decision was taken to hand-over complete responsibility for the work to the local Congolese church. Henceforward the African church leaders would be in charge and any new missionaries coming out to Congo would be under the authority of the Africans not the field leader. It was such a happy Conference - we had no idea of what lay ahead.

A few weeks later on June 30th, 1960 the Belgian Congo received its independence and became the Republic of Congo with Patrice Lumumba as its first prime minister. On Independence Day there were 2,600 Protestant missionaries in the country. In less than 50 years the church in Congo had been well established. Western missionary societies had risen to C.T. Studd's challenge. One year later Lumumba died. The Simba uprising that followed brought hostage-taking, brutality, martyrdom and the withdrawal of the missionaries.

During the Conference Bobby was staying in one of the houses belonging to the Bible School and there he was badly bitten by mosquitoes - both his ankles became very swollen. Now, while I had suffered regular bouts of malaria ever since we arrived in Congo, Bobby only had the one attack when he first came out. He was always strong and healthy. Anyway, as soon as we got back to Lubutu down he went with severe malarial fever. He became so weak that we asked for the Belgian doctor in Lubutu to come out to the station - but he was too busy. Eventually after weeks in bed his temperature began to fall and he started to get about, but whenever he tried to preach or do any building work he would pour with perspiration. The Mission had intended that we should stay on in the South and help with the new Bible School, but since Bobby was so unwell it was decided that we should return to Malingwia as soon as the Taylors got back from New Zealand and had settled in.

It was towards the end of 1960 just after the Taylors returned to Lubutu for their second term that unrest and rebellion broke out further south and began to spread northwards. When news of the trouble reached Lubutu, three Belgian officials came to the mission station to tell us that they were evacuating the European women and children to Rwanda and they advised us to join their convoy. Now that the Congo was independent the Congolese thought that the Belgians were exploiting them and that they could manage better without them. We talked the matter over with the Taylors and the Wallers - and the Taylors announced that they would be staying - even though they had four young children. Miss Harman and Mrs. Harrison down at Molita decided to do the same - they had devoted their lives to the Congo. Four years later they were all arrested at Lowa by the Simbas. All of them including the children were badly treated. They were taken to Stanleyville and imprisoned. In November 1964 Muriel Harman and Cyril Taylor were among those lined up against a wall and mown down by a machine gun. The Taylor's two young sons Murray and Barry only escaped the bullets because they fell to the ground and feigned death. They then ran to the room where their mother lay badly injured, and said: "Dad is now with Jesus." *

But to get back to 1960, on the night of November 21st a thief broke into our bungalow and stole my sewing machine plus Bobby's pen and dictionary. As we prayed together about the situation we both felt drawn back to the North to Malingwia. It was only when we reached Ibambi that we learned that many of our colleagues had already left for home because of the unrest - Mr. and Mrs. English from Malingwia, Mr. and Mrs. David Davies from Nala, Dr. and Mrs. John Harris from Nebobongo, Mr. and Mrs. Albert Moore from Ibambi itself. When we reached Malingwia it was quiet enough but there was an uneasy atmosphere. Bobby was still experiencing frequent bouts of weakness. Every time he preached he would pour with perspiration.

It was shortly after we had entered the new year that Bobby decided to go to Buta for supplies. We had heard of shortages of basic imported goods and decided to get stocked-up with provisions - especially with petrol so that we could keep mobile. Very early one morning Bobby drove up to Buta in the van. He had just finished loading some big 200 litre drums of petrol into the van when a terrible feeling of weakness came over him. He didn't know how he was going to get back to Malingwia. Just then a young African

---

* A detailed account of the W.E.C. martyrs was recorded by Len Moules in "This was no accident" (W.E.C. 1966)

Christian nurse who was working at the local hospital came along. They got into conversation and Bobby told him how ill he was feeling. The African said, "Look, lets go and find the doctor". So they searched until they found him in the "Hollandaise" shop. Then the doctor took Bobby round to the hospital and gave him an injection which made him feel better. When Bobby described his symptoms the doctor was puzzled but he said that he was very ill and strongly advised him to return to England for specialist treatment. The doctor added that in his opinion things were not going to get any easier in the Congo and that it would be wise for us to leave while we could. "There's trouble coming", he .said, "and then we may not be able to treat you".

When Bobby got back from Buta we sent a runner down to Ibambi with this information and told him to await instructions from the field committee. The runner went back and forth a few times and then it was decided to bring us down to Ibambi where the Mission's own doctor could examine Bobby. Jim Grainger the acting field leader was still at Ibambi and he decided that Pat Holdaway should come to Ibambi with us rather than leave her on the station alone. Frank Cripps came up in the mission car for us. We packed just those few essentials that could be carried in the car and Frank drove us out of Malingwia. It was just as if we were going on a shopping trip. Neither of us had any idea that it was for the last time. All our books and equipment were left behind. Would we have left had we known? Perhaps it was better that way.

Dr. Helen Roseveare came across from Nebobongo to examine Bobby. She too couldn't understand the recurring bouts of weakness he was experiencing but she agreed that he was seriously ill and thought that his heart might be fatally weakened if they continued. "That doctor at Buta in right", she said, "you ought to go home".

So it was decided to evacuate us back to England for medical treatment. How disappointed we both were! We were only eighteen months into our third term, the revival was still very much in evidence, the work was flourishing and we wanted to be part of it. Another couple left Ibambi with us. Mr. and Mrs. White from Opienge. Mr. White was a skilled builder who had built large brick churches at Ibambi and then at Opienge. They were a lovely Christian couple who had done a great work at Opienge and at Bomili, but they had two or three young children and Mrs. White wasn't very well.

Frank Cripps drove all of us to Uganda where we were to catch a flight back to Britain.   Bobby was feeling very weak and ill and couldn't get out of the car when we reached the frontier. The border guards were so rough and aggressive - there was such an evil spirit among them. One big soldier came over to Bobby brandishing his rifle and began pummelling him on the chest. "You're not ill" he kept saying. We thought they were going to shoot us. However, we reached Kampala safely and Bobby was admitted to hospital for tests. They were trying to get his blood pressure down ready for the flight home.

Then at the end of January we left Kampala on a plane bound for London. It was our very first flight. Had we known that we would never set foot in Africa again we would never have got on the aeroplane. Our hearts were in the Congo and we were expecting to return as soon as Bobby had recovered. As the plane roared along the runway then rose into the sky we watched the ground rushing past and beneath us -we were seeing Africa for the last time.

•••

"And we know that all things work together for good to them that love God, to them who are the called according to His purpose."
Romans 8: 28.

Chapter Fourteen

Another Door Opens

❖

LEN MOULES WAS WAITING AT HEATHROW AND DROVE US TO SOUTH NORWOOD. BY THAT TIME BOBBY WAS SO ill that he was lying across the back seat of the car. We half carried him into Headquarters and put him to bed. In the afternoon Joy arrived. She was on teaching practice from Southlands College at a school somewhere in Surrey and they had given her time off. She was shocked to see Dad lying so weak and ill. We were just as shocked to hear her news.

Six weeks earlier on December 21st the Lord had taken my sister Daisy to glory. It had happened very suddenly. Joy's letter never reached us. It had been the last day of term at Leominster Junior School. Daisy had come home very tired. The Young Warriors were carol singing around the town that evening but Daisy had felt too tired to go with them. Joy was away that evening to a meeting in Malvern where she was to give her testimony. "I'll be praying for you", promised Daisy. Uncle Fred went with the carol singers. When he got back and went upstairs Daisy was just passing away. Amidst her sorrow Joy could see the Lord's goodness. Daisy's work was done. Joy had been nurtured through to adulthood - and then, within weeks of losing Daisy, her own parents were home.

Joy planned to find a teaching post in London after she qualified in the summer of 1961. However she couldn't bear to think of her Uncle Fred living alone in that large flat above the shop. So she found a teaching post locally in Ludlow near Leominster. Before the end of her first term she was engaged to Thane Seager the son of the Headmaster of Leominster Junior School.

While we were in London Joy was able to come over most days. One afternoon I went to Paddington Station to meet Robert. One of his teachers had brought him up on the train from Swansea. Robert was surprised that his Dad wasn't with me. He ran into the bedroom at Highland Road and hugged Bobby telling him that the Bible College students had held a night of prayer for him.

John Harris was working at the Mildmay Mission Hospital before going on to India to study recent advances in leprosy treatment pioneered by his cousin, Dr. Paul Brand. The Mission asked him to take a look at Bobby. After a thorough examination he too was puzzled by this continuing weakness. Once the fever is over and your temperature has gone down you usually feel better. Dr. Harris agreed that Bobby was seriously ill and said that he must get away for a long and complete rest. So it was arranged that we should go to Leominster where my Brother-in-law was only too pleased to have our company.

Winnie Davies was staying at W.E.C. H.Q. while we were there. She had served in the Congo as a nurse since 1946 working with Mrs. Moules at the Leprosarium. Now she was waiting to return after furlough. Things were so uncertain at that time - some Missionaries were coming out and some were trying to get back. Winnie asked our opinion and Bobby said that he didn't think the trouble would last. "It will soon pass" he told her. Perhaps that was wishful thinking because we too wanted to get back. Shortly afterwards Winnie returned to Opienge to continue a medical work that she had begun before Independence. Following the death of Patrice Lumumba in February 1961, his followers were trained in guerilla warfare, which erupted in August 1964, the guerilla army being known as "the Simbas". For thirty-four months the rebel army marched her from place to place using her skills as a nurse and midwife until finally on May 27th 1967, she couldn't keep up with the fleeing soldiers any longer and so they shot her[*]

Fred Gurney was overjoyed to see us again and we spent some weeks with him in Leominster. Then we went on to Norton to my brother Joe. We stayed at Black Patch Farm for the rest of 1961. By the end of the year Bobby was getting stronger and feeling better. We started deputation ministry early in 1962. News from the Congo was very bad. Persecution of Christians was spreading, missionaries were being arrested and ill-treated, it was clear that we could not go back. It wasn't only the Europeans who suffered. The Simba Rebellion was an evil, devilish affair. African Christians suffered just as much at the hands of those Simbas. When the rebels reached Malingwia our African Christians were forced into the forest. There they almost starved to death. Only when the Simbas were defeated did they come out of the forest - all skin and bone.

During the Revival Dudu once remarked that God had sent it for a special purpose. "He is either preparing us for Jesus' return or for persecution", he prophesied. Dudu was a big strong man. When the Simbas reached Komo where he was pastor they demanded that he give them his beautiful eighteen year-old daughter. Dudu refused their wicked demands outright and stood in front of his daughter protecting her. There was a struggle. He managed to hold them off long enough for her to escape into the forest. Then they shot him.

When Dr. Helen Roseveare revisited Malingwia in 1989 three young African Christians had just graduated from the Bible School and were about to become pastors in the Church of Zaire. Helen was able to attend their dedication service. Pastor Mattiasi gave the commissioning address. "What a challenge he gave them!" she reported.

As we were passing in and out of our WEC British headquarters in the course of our deputation ministry we began to hear talk of France. A young couple Leslie and Eva Housen - who had originally been accepted for Congo were now at Tournon south of Lyons. Their original idea had been to awake interest among French

---

[*] A biography of Winnie Davies was published the following year. See David M. Davies, "The Captivity and Triumph of Winnie Davies" (London, 1968, Hodder and Stoughton)

Christians in mission and establish a base from which the French would send missionaries, to French-speaking countries, but the longer they stayed in France the more they realised that it was as much a mission field as the Congo.

The Housens wrote urging W.E.C. to send missionaries to central France and suggested that some of the experienced senior missionaries who couldn't return to Congo might find a useful ministry there. Albert and Olive Moore went over first. Albert knew someone connected with the International Mission to Miners which had workers in France and they put him in touch with their missionary at Carvin near Lille, John Hodson. John was proposing to open-up a new work at Courrières and needed help. So it was agreed that the Mission to Miners would become the 'Stepping stone' upon which W.E.C. would enter France and that John Hodson would help our missionaries to settle in. John rented a derelict bistro in the forecourt of the disused railway station at Courrières and the Moores moved into the large apartment above the café. Once renovated it would be ideal for meetings.

After a few months Albert and Olive were acclimatised and wanted to move to central France which the Housens said was a needy region. A new W.E.C. field was created with Leslie Housen as field leader. Then Len Moules our General Secretary put it to us, "Would we take the Moore's place at Courrières?"

My heart was still in the Congo. I continued to nurture a hope that it would become possible for us to return. I didn't want to go to France, I didn't feel led to France or have any emotional commitment towards France. Yet my French was quite good - better than Bobby's! A lot of my teaching in the Congo had been in French because we had to follow the Belgian curriculum. Bobby felt sure that the Lord was leading us forward and so - very reluctantly - I followed my husband because that was my duty. Within a few weeks I was experiencing such contentment and peace and I knew that France was exactly the right place for us.

Shortly before we crossed the Channel in September 1962 another milestone in our family history was passed. On August 28th Joy and Thane were married. At that time Leominster Baptist Church was without a pastor so it all worked out wonderfully well. Joy's

Uncle Fred gave her away while Bobby conducted the service and married them. The Church was filled with uncles and aunts, nephews and nieces - including my Brother Jack who was now Pastor of an F.I.E.C. Church in Cheltenham. After their honeymoon Joy and Thane went to live in Holland where Thane was working for the Shell Oil Company - and we went to live in Courrières.

John Hodson had re-named the bistro "La Phare" (The Lighthouse). It had stood empty and neglected for several years and needed a lot of work to make it habitable. Albert had begun renovating the flat. The Moores were still there when we arrived and they helped us to become familiar with the town before moving on down to Vichy. In December Joy and Thane drove across from The Hague to visit us. "La Phare" seemed so cold and dingy, poor and miserable, compared with Leominster or London or Lubutu - but we were not miserable - it was the place the Lord had provided.

For fourteen months we helped John Hodson - taking meetings and learning to speak French as it was spoken in France. Ruth Brain - an American with Bible Christian Union stayed with us and helped with the childrens' meetings. It was this time that a new work developed at Billybercleau. A keen young French Christian, Jack Ganechon, had opened his home for meetings and God was blessing his ministry. The Miners' Mission had a prefabricated building at Libercourt which had been intended for use in outreach among the many Algerians and North Africans living in that district but the work was very slow. So it was decided to move the building to Billybercleau. Jack obtained a site and permission from the authorities and Bobby spent many Saturdays working on that building with Monsieur Chateau, Etienne Vagoda and other Christian miners who had given their day off to serve the Lord.

In the summer of 1963 we held a tent mission in Courrières. A team of students from London Bible College helped us and Robert was over from Swansea. Shortly after that we moved down to central France. The Moores were living in a rented farmhouse near Commentry so we stayed with them until we could find a place of our own. We borrowed their ancient Citroen car and searched around the district for somewhere to live. Eventually we came to the town of Ebreuil and were directed to a house. A young man came out and said, "Mum and Dad have a little cottage out in the country". He had a sister who was learning English and had been to England. She was thrilled to meet some English people. Bobby said "Will you show us it?" So they took us out to see their parents' cottage. It was in a little hamlet called Villeneuve about three miles from Ebreuil right out in the country - there were only about ten houses. We said "This would be ideal". They said "Come tomorrow and talk to our Father and Mother". When they told their parents that English Protestants wanted to rent the cottage the Mother was strongly against it. "What does it matter if they're Protestants?" the boy asked. "I'm going to see the priest first", his mother replied. Monsieur Goyeau was a business man. He didn't care who they let it to. Anyway when we called the next day Madame Goyeau said, "I'm not going to make any arrangements until the priest gives me his permission". (There is a large Roman Catholic convent in Ebreuil). The Priest's only comment was, "Well, they're better than the Communists". So the Goyeaus agreed to let us rent their cottage - and that was our home for the next seven years.

•••

".. and after the earthquake a fire. but the LORD was not in the fire: and after the fire a still small voice".
I Kings 19: 12.

Chapter Fifteen

Generation to Generation

❖

OUR HOUSE WAS A TYPICAL FRENCH COUNTRY COTTAGE - WHITEWASHED CLAY WALLS, RED TILED ROOF - THREE rooms downstairs, two up. Before Ivy and I moved in Monsieur Goyeau had it renovated and installed a bathroom upstairs. Over the years I was able to make more improvements. In place of the outside earth closet a proper toilet was put in. For a time ours was the only house in Villeneuve with a flush toilet. One of the downstairs rooms we turned into a third bedroom and I used another as a study. Alongside the cottage was a large barn which served as a garage, and there was a big back garden where I grew vegetables.

The people of Villeneuve were very friendly. About a dozen families lived in the hamlet and we quickly got to know them all - especially the Touveron family. They were farmers. Every day we walked down to their farm to get our milk. There was an old grandmother, Madame Touveron who was a widow, and her two children: Jean, who ran the farm, and Bernardette who was studying to be a lawyer in Clermont-Ferrand. They were a devout Roman Catholic family yet Madame Touveron was so open and interested - and so was her daughter when she was home from university. They welcomed us into their home and were delighted to hear the Scriptures read - and Madame Touveron would pray with us. Very soon after our arrival we began regular meetings in their house and on a Sunday we gathered there for worship with the Touverons, Madame Blacré', and Monsieur and Madame Vivier - all from Villeneuve. How they loved to sing and read and pray with us! It was such a joy to hear Madame Touveron open her heart to the Lord in prayer. Madame Touveron had many friends in the district; she made openings for us and even told us which people to visit.

Madame Vivier was our first convert in France - her husband worked on the Touveron's farm. Soon after that she was diagnosed as suffering from Parkinson's Disease. She was only in her 50's. The people of Villneuve superstitiously remarked, "Look what happens when you get involved with Protestants!".

Madame Vivier, however, remained bright and cheerful despite her increasing disability. This so impressed her old Mother - who had been very much against us - that she too opened her heart to the Lord before her daughter went to be with Him.

We visited every house in the district going from door to door distributing tracts and other Christian literature. For transport we inherited the Moore's ancient Citroen. Its two front seats were so worn and loose that they were quite dangerous, but one day I noticed a couple of Citroen front seats on the rubbish dump at Ebreuil. They were better than ours! So I repaired and fitted them into our car. The two 'useless' car seats were made into comfortable chairs for our parlour.

The nearest town after Ebreuil was Gannat about fifteen miles from Villeneuve. Over the years we soaked that town in literature. One of the most effective pieces was a calendar which we sold from door to door. It had a tear-off text and message (in French of course) for each day. By 1970 they were to be found hanging in homes and shops throughout the district. Each piece of literature carried our name and address. One day shortly after our first distribution in Gannat we received a letter from a lady living there asking us to visit her. She added that for many years she had longed to have a Bible and know its teaching. When we called round we found that the writer was an elderly lady - the widow of a lawyer who had been quite an important person in the town. Madame Menon had a great spiritual hunger for the Word of God. So we promised to call every week, read the Bible with her and explain the Scriptures to her. Within a few weeks she was seeking the Saviour. We explained the way of salvation to her and - do you know - she came right through to faith in Christ - truly born again. Then she introduced us to a friend - a German lady - who was a Protestant. That lady and her husband were also seeking Christian fellowship and instruction. Madame Menon would bring in her friends and neighbours when we came for Bible study and prayer.

A year or so afterwards Madame Menon became ill and was taken into hospital in Vichy. The nuns were amazed at her faith. We visited her regularly and told her that we were praying for her recovery. "NO", she said. "Don't do that. I want to go to heaven". Madame Menon's was the first funeral I conducted in France.

God gave us the ability to get into homes. We received so many invitations that we were kept busy every day from morning to night distributing literature and holding little house meetings. While going from door to door in Ebreuil we met an architect and his wife. They were most interested and opened their home for meetings. Then Madame Touveron introduced us to an elderly lady in Ebreuil who was a devout Roman Catholic but hungry for the Word of God. So interest was increasing and the work developing. Then the priest at Ebreuil began to get worried. He wrote in the parish magazine,

"These are good people but they cannot give you all that the Roman Catholic Church does: they don't pray to Mary, they don't pray for your dead, and they don't believe in a lot that the Church teaches. Although they are good people they cannot teach you as much as we can."

But that only turned our friends against him. They said, "The Protestants do respect Mary but they don't worship her". We used their Catholic Douai New Testament in our studies and they were amazed to see that there was hardly any difference from our French Protestant version. Gradually light was spreading, understanding was growing.

There was one young priest in the area who was sympathetic towards our work. He had a sister who was a nun, his mother was a devout Roman Catholic but his father was a Protestant. He had a meeting in one of the houses in his parish. One day he invited us to come and explain to his people how Protestantism began. So I told them about Martin Luther and how one day when he was a monk God opened his understanding of the Scriptures and he realised that he couldn't be saved by good works but only by faith in Jesus Christ. When I finished that priest turned to his people and said, "Had the Pope listened to Martin Luther there would have been no division between Catholics and Protestants". He became very friendly with us, but when the Bishop heard about it he was suddenly moved to another parish.

While we were at Villeneuve I passed my driving test - I'd never needed a licence in the Congo. After that we ran a sort of voluntary taxi service from Villeneuve taking people into Ebreuil to the doctor or hospital - or taking the Rifaufs, who lived in the farm opposite, to market to sell their rabbits. A few weeks after I passed my test, we had news from the Congo about the martyrs.

We had been in Villeneuve three years when W.E.C. informed us that they were sending two young ladies, Phemie Dowling and Margaret Jones to join us. They had just completed language study in Paris. We found them a flat in Gannat. Phemie and Margaret were fluent in French - unlike us older missionaries who had picked the language up as we went along. They started visitation and then things began to develop very quickly - they had some amazing openings. A children's work was begun and before long Phemie and Margaret had a crowd of children coming to their flat each week. Then we had a Scottish young man come to us from language school in Paris. Matt Paton was an expert in French - as he went around with us the locals were amazed at his fluency. The architect and his family at Ebreuil were greatly blessed through Matt's ministry in their home. Matt became engaged to Margaret. After they were married they were able to buy a house in Gannat. They turned the ground floor into a meeting room and lived upstairs. Regular Sunday services were held there with a good number attending - as well as the childrens' work at which they were very gifted. A church was forming in Gannat - things were going very well indeed. Meanwhile, the Housens had left Tournon and returned to England and so Albert Moore was serving as our field leader.

Every year we would spend a month on furlough in Britain usually at Black Patch Farm where we would meet up with Robert. He would come out to us in France for at least part of his other school holidays. We also saw Joy and Thane regularly each year. They and their two little boys would drive down from Holland to spend their summer holiday with us in central France. Mark Seager - our first grandchild - was born in 1963 - and Kevin two years later. In the summer of 1968 they were on holiday with us at Villeneuve - Mark was five at the time. One day I drove into Vichy for some shopping and took Mark with me. As we drove along Mark was singing,

"Yes Jesus loves me, yes, Jesus loves me,

Yes Jesus loves me. The Bible tells me so".

I looked over to him and asked "Mark, you know that Jesus loves you - but do YOU love him?"

For a little while he sat quietly thinking. Then all of a sudden he said, "Grandad, will you stop the car?"

"Why?" I asked.

"I want to tell Jesus that I do love Him," Mark answered.

So I said, "Mark, there's no need to stop the car. You can tell Jesus as we go along that you do love Him and that you want Him to be your Saviour".

So he prayed in the car as we drove into Vichy. What struck me was that as soon as we got back home Mark ran to Joy and said,

"Mum, I'm a Christian. I've told Jesus that I love Him. I've prayed with Grandad that He will become my Saviour".

Then he turned to three year-old Kevin and asked, "Kevin, won't you tell Jesus that you love Him?"

Kevin feeling contrary said, "No I won't!"

Then Mark began to cry. Joy put her arm round him and said, "Don't cry, Mark. We will pray for Kevin that he will come to understand what it means to love Jesus, and that one day he will ask Jesus to be his Saviour"

It wasn't long afterwards that the family moved to America (in January 1970) because Thane got a job with The World Bank in Washington, D.C. Initially they went to live in Maryland. There they joined an active church with a very good Sunday School.

One day, Joy was doing her housework, when five year old Kevin began tugging at her skirt and saying ...."but I can't sing very well."

What's the matter, Kevin?", Joy asked.

Eventually everything became clear when Kevin said, "I want to ask Jesus into my heart .... but I can't sing very well."

Kevin had remembered Mark's conversion in France and the singing of "Yes, Jesus loves me".

Joy assured him that he didn't need to sing - he could just pray - and so there and then she led little Kevin through to faith in the Lord Jesus Christ.

One of the most thrilling experiences of my life took place in England a few years later when I heard all four grandchildren give their testimony. For the first time I heard Mark tell his version of events during that car ride into Vichy years before. In a later chapter I'll tell you about that memorable Sunday morning.

•••

"One generation shall praise Thy Works to another, and shall declare Thy mighty acts."
Psalm 145: 4

Chapter Sixteen

Back to Courrières

❖

MY GRANDSON MARK WAS CONVERTED IN THE SUMMER OF 1968. THE FOLLOWING YEAR, OUR SON ROBERT LEFT Emmanuel Grammar School. Like his sister he had decided to become a school teacher. The headmaster at Swansea advised him to apply to Portsmouth Teacher Training College where there were several Christian lecturers. Ivy's youngest brother Richard was a minister there - so Robert applied for a place at the College and was accepted. In September 1969 he moved to Portsmouth and soon afterwards joined Paulsgrove Baptist Church where his Uncle Dick was the minister - Robert is still in active membership at Paulsgrove today.

We had been at Villeneuve for eight years and the witness was now well established in the district. Then, one day early in 1971 we had a letter from John Hodson asking if we would be prepared to come back to Courrières. John was returning to England to take over the Miners' Mission work at Aylsham near Canterbury. While we had been down in central France the work, which had only just begun in Courrières when we arrived, had so prospered that the

Miners' Mission had bought a large house there and the Hodsons had moved across from Carvin.

Together we prayed over this letter and then shared it with our fellow workers and with headquarters in London. All were agreed that this was the Lord's leading and so W.E.C. seconded us to the Miners' Mission to work with John Hodson again. In June 1971 we left Villeneuve and returned to Courrières where we stayed with the Hodsons until they returned to England the following September. The church in Courrières met in the house too.

Just before John left France we had a visit from Jacques Ganechon. The work at Billybercleau was developing - believers were being added to the church and there had been some baptisms. Jack was needing help and so every Tuesday night we went over to the Bible study group that met in the hut we had transported from Libercourt.

One day Marie Di Vicenzo - one of our church members who lived in Carvin came to us and said, "I would like you to come and visit one of my neighbours. We have given her a Bible". We drove over to Carvin to see Giselle but we found that her daughter was more interested in the Gospel than she was. Giselle's husband had left her and she was taken up with her troubles. Her daughter Anne was engaged to Jacques. I invited them to a meeting at the Baptist Church in Lens and then they both started coming to our meetings in Courrières. After a few months of teaching, both Anne and Jacques were truly born again - and then we had the joy of baptising them. My first wedding at Courrières was that of Anne and Jacques.

Giselle also had three sons - all three had very poor eyesight. One day she said to me, "Will you come and start a Bible study group in my home?" Gradually those three boys - Philippe, François and Armand - came through to faith in Christ. François could hardly see at all but he was very musical. We got him to a music teacher at Carvin, she was amazed at his ability and straight-away took him on as a pupil. François is now a professional musician. All three brothers have married Christian girls and are going on with the Lord.

There was another lovely Christian family in Courrières, the Vagodas. They had two sons and a daughter. Étienne Vagoda was an electrician in the coal mine. Both Étienne, his brother Jacques, and his sister were Christians - and we married both brothers to lovely Christian girls. So we saw Christian families being created in Courrières.

Before I go any further I'd like to tell you something more about the Di Vicenzo family. They were Italians - Maria's husband had come up to work in the mines. They were strong Roman Catholics when they moved into Carvin. One day one of our young lads was going from door to door distributing Christian literature. When he reached Maria's house she tried to put him off saying,

"I haven't got time for that. My little daughter is seriously ill with asthma."

He asked, "Would you like me to come in and pray with you for her?"

Maria was so taken aback that all she could say was, "Yes! Come on in."

Then that young boy prayed earnestly that Leila would be healed, and the Lord heard his prayer. She recovered from the attack and gradually was restored to full health. As a result Mrs. Di Vicenzo came along to John Hodson's meetings in Carvin bringing her two daughters - and all three were converted. Leila and her younger sister Rosa became bright, keen Christians. Both are now married to Christian husbands and have children of their own.

Another young Christian at Courrières was Shafir. Her parents were Algerian Moslems with a large family but all the children came to our Sunday school and Shafir became a Christian. At first she experienced terrible opposition from her family - even death threats. A marriage was arranged for her, but Shafir ran away from home and got a job in Lille. Eventually she married a Christian boy and is now reconciled with her family.

In April 1974 we had a visit from Dr. John Harris and his wife Elsie who were taking their two children on a trip to the South of France before returning to Zaire (Congo) after furlough. They spent a couple of nights with us in Courrières and we were able to catch up on all the news from Malingwia.

The Lord was prospering the work at Billybercleau as well. There had been several baptismal services there. One young missionary couple from a non-Baptist background were so impressed that they too asked for baptism - and so Jack Ganechon and I baptised them by immersion at the next baptismal service at Billybercleau. After they had completed their language study they went on to serve the Lord somewhere in Africa.

It was during our fifth year at Courrières that we met Malcolm and Lyn Slater at the W.E.C. field conference. They had been working down at Clermont-Ferrand on their own and had found it difficult to make contacts. They were very disheartened and ready to give up. Shortly afterwards the young Baptist pastor at Lens came to us and said, "Would you have any young couples in your mission who would like to come and work with me?". Immediately it occurred to me that the Slaters would benefit from working in association with a French pastor. I mentioned their name and he was very enthusiastic. So we put it to Malcolm and Lyn and to the field committee. It was agreed that they should move up to Béthune where the Lens Baptist pastor had a second charge and gain experience as his assistants. He was such a help to them and soon they became established. Eventually the French pastor moved to Germany to teach in a Baptist theological college - his wife was German - and then Malcolm and Lyn took over responsibility for both churches. Later a young French school teacher, Thierry de la Longue, became the pastor at Béthune. Malcolm, Lyn and their three daughters settled so successfully into the ministry at Lens that they have resigned from W.E.C., joined the French Baptist Church and taken out French citizenship. Now they are pastoring two churches at Papignè.

Another young W.E.C. couple, Drew and Joy Wilkinson, were also finding it difficult to settle in central France. So we suggested that they should come up to Courrières and work under Jacques Ganechon at Billybercleau. Again the field committee agreed to our suggestion. Then we went to the town hall and saw the mayor and explained our need for accommodation for the Wilkinsons and their two boys. Immediately he agreed to provide them with a nice flat in Courrières so then we arranged for their boys to attend the local school. So the Wilkinson family came to help us - and soon we could see that God was blessing and using them in Courrières - especially in the flourishing children's work. They were both very good at French - far more fluent than ourselves. There was plenty of work for all of us. Every Wednesday I would go out with the van and bring loads of children into the meeting. Once I was stopped by the local gendarme and warned for cramming too many kids into the van. Leila and Roa Di Vincenzo would help us. In all three places - the Patons at Gannat, the Slaters at Béthune, the Wilkinsons at Courrières - their children were a tremendous help breaking down barriers and making contacts through their school friends.

We also worked with Peter Wheeler, a Brethren missionary who had a touring Bible exhibition. We were able to arrange for the exhibition to be held at the town hall - the mayor opened it and we presented him with a Bible. Every summer a team from the London Bible College would come across and help us with a mission. We had absolute liberty. We had a stall in the market and sold masses of Gospel literature. Even the Roman Catholic priest at Courrières was very friendly. He invited us to come and talk to his young people. We asked him if we could give them some Scripture Gift Mission literature. "Sure", he said, "Let them have it".

Once a year the mayor of Courrières gave a dinner for the town's senior citizens. One year he invited us! After the meal the mayor turned to Ivy and said, "Tell us something about the days when you lived in the Congo, Madame Milliken". So Ivy, who was very fluent in French and can always tell a story, spoke about our life in the villages before the War. After she had finished everyone clapped. The priest, who was sitting opposite us and had listened intently, leaned across and said "Madame Milliken is a guileless woman. I have enjoyed all that she said".

By 1979 we had been seventeen years in France. During that time we had seen the Patons established at Gannat, the Slaters at Lens and the Wilkinsons at Courrières. Three keen capable couples with young families and great fluency in French. We had worked ourselves out of a job - which was what W.E.C. had planned when they sent us across the Channel in 1962.

We were beginning to wonder what the Lord wanted us to do next when we were approached by Dr. Shewell-Cooper the chairman of the Miners Mission. He told us that John Hodson was leaving the Mission and returning to Birmingham and that they needed an experienced couple to serve at Aylsham. "Would we take over from John?" he inquired.

As we prayed about it we felt sure that this was the Lord's leading because the work at Courrières would not be left unattended. In fact it would be left in younger and more capable hands than ours. Here, then, was our next step - the Lord's clear call to return to England.

•••

"As we have therefore opportunity, let us do good unto all, especially unto them who are of the household of faith".
Galatians 6: 10

Chapter Seventeen

Aylsham Finale

❖

OUR SEVENTIETH BIRTHDAYS HAD BEEN CELEBRATED IN COURRIÈRES - SO WE WERE WELL INTO OUR SEVENTY-first year when we moved across the Channel to settle in England. During his eight years at Aylsham John Hodson had steadily built up the Mission - especially the children's work. One of his daughters was a gifted musician and was used to be a great help and blessing among the young people. She had a tent and would have girls from the Mission camping in the manse back garden - and there she would lead them to the Lord. Three in particular - Annette, Christine and Alison - became really committed Christians.

While we were waiting for the manse to be vacated we stayed with Ivy's niece Clarice and her husband. Do you remember little Clarice Roberts who Ivy led to the Lord in the farm-house at Rock near Newtown when she was just four years old - I told you about her in Chapter 9? Well, now she was Mrs. Michael Wilcock, had two little girls, and in God's strange providence her home was in a neighbouring village to Aylsham. Michael was an executive with the Electricity Board and a committed Christian. He was helping

Mrs. Drew run a little chapel in their village. When they went out to meetings we would babysit for them. Then the Miners' Mission organised a removal van to collect our furniture from Courrières and bring it to the manse. I went over with the van and spent one final night in France with Jack Ganechon and then we moved into the Aylsham manse.

There was a flourishing Sunday school at the Mission but no morning service. Soon after we arrived the members asked if we would develop a regular morning worship service after the Sunday School, which we did. Ivy led the Tuesday ladies meeting - they were a lovely group of ladies - my wife got on with them so well - she lived for that meeting. Annette Neery and her sister Christine taught in the Sunday school - and Alison helped Ivy with the tiny tots. The three girls also formed a singing trio and when our organist moved away from the village Christine took over as the Mission's organist.

Every Tuesday evening we had a Bible study and of course we did a lot of visiting and then there was the preparation of messages for the Sunday services. We were kept very busy. Our French connections were maintained through frequent visits by groups of young people from Courrières, Billybercleau and Lens. So we saw the work growing.

I had been driving a car or van first in the Congo and then in France for over forty years but I wasn't qualified to drive in Britain because I didn't have a British licence. So in January 1980 I had to take a U.K. driving test in order to get a proper licence. By this time I was into my 72nd year and I took the test in crowded Canterbury wondering what would happen if the examiner failed me. The Lord knew we needed transport - I passed!

About a year after we arrived in Aylsham I had the joy of leading Mark Saddington to the Lord. It happened this way: Annette Neary worked as a hairdresser alongside Mark and they began to go out together. Annette brought him along to the Sunday evening services and I could see that an interest in the things of God was developing. On one occasion Mark admitted that he had never even seen a Bible before he started attending the Mission with Annette. Then during our Good Friday meeting he fell under real conviction of sin.

After the service he was hanging around looking miserable so I went up and asked, "Mark, what's the matter?"

He replied, "You know I want to marry Annette but she won't marry me because I'm not a Christian. Well, I do want to become a Christian but not just because of Annette. I want it to be real."

And so I counselled him and Mark gave his life to the Lord. The following summer we held a Baptismal service in the sea at Dover - Mark, Annette, Christine and Alison were baptised with all the Aylsham Mission folk and a crowd of holiday-makers watching. Before they were baptised each gave their testimony on the beach. Then Michael, Clarice's husband, who is a tall fellow waded out into the sea with them and performed the baptisms. A few months later Mark and Annette were married in Aylsham Mission and I had the privilege of conducting their wedding. When our Sunday school superintendent had to go into hospital and afterwards felt she should hand over to someone else, Mark and Annette took her place. Today they have three children and still live in Aylsham and have started a house group in their home. They are connected with Lyddon Baptist Church where Annette's sister Christine is the organist - she too married a fine Christian fellow; we were invited back to Aylsham for their wedding.

Altogether I married four couples at the Mission. Alison Harding and her fiancée Keith were among them. Keith was a technician in the R.A.F. and was stationed at a base somewhere in the North of England. His father was a miner at Aylsham. They had been seeing each other on and off for about six years, but like her friend Annette Neary, Alison wouldn't marry a non-Christian. Then one day Keith was home on leave, came along to a service at the Mission and was soundly converted - you can always tell when they are really through to faith in Christ for salvation. They bought a house near his R.A.F. base and were married just before the Gulf War. Soon afterwards Keith was sent out to Kuwait to service the aircraft.

Another great joy was to witness the restoration to our fellowship of Fred Bowley. Fred had been in the army and had married an Aylsham girl. When he was discharged he became a miner. They had two daughters and a son who all came to our Sunday school. Fred had been converted under John Hodson's ministry but had gone right back. The Lord laid it on our hearts to visit him and we had a serious talk with him. We prayed together, Fred repented, made things right, and was restored. One Sunday he stood at the front of the mission and confessed to us all that he had backslidden and had not been all that he should have been but the Lord had forgiven him. Fred became such a faithful member. He never missed a meeting. In fact he would come along to the manse for extra Bible study - we went through the Book of Daniel together. Fred still lives in Aylsham and belongs to the local Baptist Church - he writes to us regularly.

Now that we were living in England we were able to see Robert more often. He was teaching in a secondary school near Portsmouth and would drive up to Kent during the school holidays. We would also see Joy and Thane and our grandchildren every summer, one year they would come to England the next we would go to America. It was, I think, during their first summer holiday in Aylsham that our Sunday school superintendent, Mrs. Armstrong, invited our grandchildren to come out to the front and tell their testimonies to the Sunday school. One by one Mark, Kevin, Colin and Vivian told how they had come to know the Lord Jesus - Mark during that car ride into Vichy, Kevin, Colin and Vivian (who was about the same age as Joy had been when she gave her heart to the Lord in Gwystre Chapel) at home in Virginia. All four were baptised at Reston Bible Church and are still following the Lord faithfully.

When it was our turn to cross the Atlantic we were kept so busy throughout the month away that it was no different from Aylsham or Courrières or Villeneuve. Reston is a new town just outside Washington D.C. Like all new towns it was mostly inhabited by young newly married couples when Thane and Joy moved there in 1971. The Bible Church was founded three years later by a Christian business man who was concerned that there was no evangelical witness in the town. They had called a young pastor straight from Bible college and had hired two rooms in the Sheraton Hotel for their services. When Joy and Thane began attending there were twenty-three young Christians gathering with the pastor - and not even a Sunday school for their children. Now, twenty years on, the congregation numbers around 1,800 and they have to hold three sittings for each service because their new building is already too small to accommodate everyone.

Ivy and I had so many invitations to speak at the many house fellowships and weekly home Bible studies linked to the church that Joy had to organise a diary of engagements before we arrived. Since Reston was such a young church our long Christian experience enabled us to be of use in counselling. One couple in particular come to mind. The husband had been converted at the church but his wife hadn't and then she left him. We were able to meet, talk and pray with both of them, and bring them back together. Then the wife came to the Lord; now they have two children, are a united Christian family, and the husband is one of Reston Bible Church's assistant pastors.

In March 1988 we celebrated our golden wedding anniversary. First of all Robert organised a family reunion at Aylsham and then a week later we flew to America and had a second party in the church hall at Reston. Almost every member of the Bible Church was there - and we even received a letter of congratulation from President and Mrs. Reagan. This is what they wrote:

The White House
Washington, D.C.

"We are delighted to congratulate you on your anniversary. As you celebrate the memories of your wedding day and your life together, we know how you cherish the love that has united you through the years. At this special time we wish you every happiness and send our best wishes."

May God bless you always,

Nancy Reagan and Ronald Reagan.

But that's jumping ahead. The year before our fiftieth anniversary we travelled to Northern Ireland to take part in the centenary celebrations of The Welcome Mission. In Belfast we met up with many old friends and had a reunion with the surviving members of my family - but by that time one of my closest relatives had come to live with us at Aylsham.

Looking back to Chapter I see that I never mentioned my brother Joe. He was the baby of the family - much younger than the rest of us. Joe was just a nine-year old boy when Mother died and my oldest sister Lily then took care of him. Well, Joe always loved horses and as soon as he was old enough he went into the army and joined a cavalry regiment. For a while I had been his Sunday school teacher but our paths never crossed once I left Belfast and joined W.E.C.. Anyway, just before World War 2 Joe's regiment was in the Middle East. There it was re-equipped with tanks and sent to North Africa to fight Rommel's army. Then Joe was captured by the Germans and spent the rest of the war in Italy as a prisoner of war. When the war ended he was released and discharged from the army but he couldn't settle down. Then he went to Australia where he worked as a cowboy on a cattle station in the outback for about twenty-five years. He never married. As he grew older Joe came to realise that he didn't want to end his days alone and far from his homeland. One day out of the blue we got a letter from Joe telling us that he had retired, would like to return to Britain, and asking if he could stay with us. Although Ivy had never met him and he wasn't a Christian believer she welcomed my brother into our home in the manse at Aylsham - and there he stayed.

My brother was a quiet, mild-mannered fellow - not at all antagonistic to the Gospel. He got a job working with elderly people in an old folks home. Every Friday he would make tea for us. Alison Harding would come straight to the Mission from her work as a secretary in the office of Mission Aviation Fellowship at Folkestone to help Ivy prepare for their Sunday school class - and Joe prepared tea for them. Before we moved out of the manse we found a place for Joe in a residential home. By then he was 72 - and didn't want to leave Aylsham. A few weeks later we received a letter saying that he wasn't very happy there and would we pray that he could be found a more suitable place. We all made it a matter of prayer. Shortly afterwards the Christian friends in Aylsham found him a place in a Christian home. The next letter from Joe told us very simply that he had received the Lord Jesus Christ as his Saviour and was enjoying the Christian fellowship and peaceful atmosphere of the home. When Robert took a group of his pupils on a trip to Canterbury we went with him and called in to see Joe. It was clear that he wasn't very well but what a thrill to hear him say that he was trusting Christ as his Saviour. Not long after that we heard that he had gone to be with the Lord. How thankful we were that the manse was big enough for us to take in Joe.

During our nine years in Aylsham the situation completely changed. The mines in the Kent coalfield were closing and the village was emptying. Then our church building became dangerous due to subsidence in the underground workings and was condemned. Services were discontinued but we continued to use the side hall for the Sunday school. Then the leaders of The Miners' Mission visited us and said that they felt that the Mission's mandate in the village had come to an end now that the mine had closed. They asked us to pray about the situation and seek the Lord's guidance. Not long after our golden wedding celebrations I had a slight stroke and Ivy too was not as fit as she had been a year or so earlier. Everything pointed to a move - but where?

•••

"And ye shall hallow the fiftieth year, and proclaim liberty throughout the land unto all the inhabitants thereof: it shall be a jubilee unto you; and ye shall return every man unto his possession, and ye shall return every man unto his family."
Leviticus 25: 10.

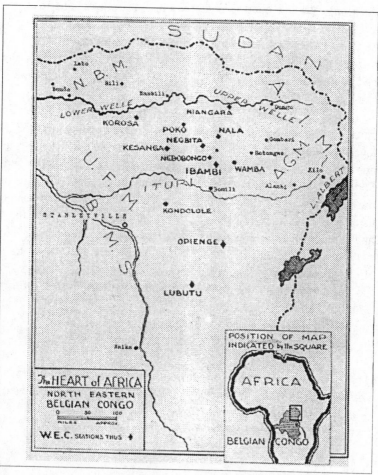

The North-Eastern Congo.

Chapter Eighteen

A Home in Hampshire

❖

IT WAS A LONG DRIVE FROM PORTSMOUTH TO KENT AND BACK FOR ROBERT WHEN HE VISITED US AT WEEKENDS. He was praying that the Lord would give us a place nearer to him - and after being separated foɪ most of our lives we too wanted to be near him.

One Sunday Robert was preaching at a Brethren assembly in Fareham and after the meeting he mentioned that he was looking for a place for his parents. One of the elders said that there was a Christian lady in Warsash who owned a furnished bungalow which she kept for missionaries on furlough - and it was vacant! So Robert got in touch with Mrs. Rombach and arranged for us to come down and visit her. Then she offered us the bungalow for a year.

We moved out of the manse at Aylsham a few days after my eightieth birthday. Robert had hired a van and brought some of the young people up from Paulsgrove. They loaded our furniture into the van and then we drove away. Our years in the village had been happy, useful years and we were sorry to be leaving - but our work was finished. Although the Miners' Mission had closed, the Church of Christ in Aylsham was very much alive - the childrens' work was in the safe hands of the Saddingtons - and a group of committed believers were meeting regularly in their house fellowship. So we drove down from Kent with hearts filled with praise to God for His goodness. When we reached Portsmouth our furniture was off-loaded into the basement of Paulsgrove Baptist Church to be stored until needed again. Then we drove on to Warsash and moved into the bungalow in Brook Lane.

On our first Sunday there we went with Mr. and Mrs. Rombach to their church Locks Heath Free Church. It was packed out with young people and very lively but we felt lost in such a large congregation. We asked Pam Rombach if there was not some small struggling cause in the neighbourhood where we could be of some help. Immediately she thought of Titchfield. The Congregational Chapel in the village had closed in the 1980's. But in 1989 about twenty Christian believers had covenanted together to re-constitute and re-build as an Independent Evangelical Church using the old chapel premises. Now they were seeking a pastor but first they had to purchase a manse. It sounded just the place for us. So the next Sunday morning we got Robert to take us over. He had a preaching engagement so he went in and asked if someone could run us back to Warsash after the service.

We felt really at home in that little fellowship. Afterwards a Christian brother introduced himself as "Charles" and said that he could give us a lift back to Warsash because he lived in that direction. Charles became such a good friend to us. He was an elderly man living on his own since his wife went into a nursing home. Twice each Sunday he would call for us and take us into Titchfield to the services and then bring us home, and then again on Tuesday evenings for the Bible study and prayer meeting. I think Charles had been quite lonely and was pleased to have our fellowship.

Titchfield Evangelical Church was clearly the Lord's place for us but we only had the bungalow for a year and didn't feel we could become full members unless we were settled in the district. The months were passing and our time at Warsash was running out. We were much in prayer about the situation, as were the church at Paulsgrove and the little group at Titchfield who were delighted to have our support. Then the Titchfield friends learned that one of the bungalows in a modern sheltered housing complex behind the chapel had suddenly become vacant. They suggested that we apply to the Housing Department and Charles offered to take us into the Council Offices in Fareham. A few days later Charles drove us into Fareham and came with us to the Housing Department. A man in the office took our details but didn't hold out much hope. He said they had a long waiting list of local people looking for accommodation. Charles replied, "God is on the throne and if God wants this couple to have that bungalow He'll get it for them". The man answered, "That may be so but I cannot give you any encouragement". We went home and really gave ourselves to prayer. A week later a lady from the department came to visit us at Warsash to take more details. We explained to her that we were retired missionaries and that our son was a school teacher at Stubbington not far from Titchfield, and if we could have that bungalow he would be so relieved. Although she didn't say anything it seemed to us that that lady was a Christian and we felt that God was going to answer prayer. A couple of days later we had a phone call telling us that the Housing Committee had decided that we could have the bungalow and would we come over to Fareham and collect the keys. Charles and Robert were over the moon when they heard the news.

At the end of February 1990 we moved into No. 26 Chapel Side or rather we were moved. First, Robert organised the hanging of curtains and laying of carpets, then he hired a van and with the help of the Paulsgrove young people brought our furniture out of the basement of the church and into the bungalow. Not many weeks later Charles went on holiday and one night he passed away in his sleep. His work had been completed and the Lord took him home.

There are twenty flats and bungalows in the complex. Ours is right by the entrance to the cul-de-sac. From our kitchen window we can see everyone coming and going - and everyone knows us! During the past four years we have visited all the residents and make a point of welcoming any new arrivals. Each Christmas we distribute Christian calendars with Scripture texts to everyone in the neighbourhood. Three of the elderly folk have come along with us to the morning service, including the lady next door, but on Sunday afternoons their families often call and take them out and they don't get back in time for church.

Our main ministry has been in Titchfield Evangelical Church especially at the mid week prayer meeting. Two years ago the church was able to obtain a manse and soon afterwards a young pastor and his family accepted the church's call to ministry in Titchfield. A lady had been soundly converted on the Sunday he first preached here. Since then we have held three baptisms but there have also been some severe setbacks when key members moved away. Our ministry has been one of encouragement both to the young pastor and to his little flock.

Our trips to Reston, Virginia have continued. In May 1992 we attended our grandson Kevin's wedding in Reston Bible Church. I was so pleased to be invited to take part in the service. Kevin and Karen are now in Spain with UFM International, having done language study at Malaga before moving on to Marbella and then Almeria to work among Moslems.* Our children and grandchildren are all serving the Lord, the missionary vision has been passed on.

Earlier this year we received a letter from Congo from Mattiasi. He is now the senior pastor in charge of the whole district - and getting on in years himself! One of his sons who was only a baby when we left the Congo is now a full-time evangelist with the Church of Congo. We also keep in touch with the Patons, Slaters and Wilkinsons in France - their children are all grown up, converted, and engaged in the Lord's work. From time to time we hear from Fred Bowley in Aylsham. The witness in the village continues - the fellowship has now linked up with the lively Baptist Church in Canterbury. The Lord's Kingdom grows - His work goes on.

So here we are in 1994 living in our compact, convenient, centrally-heated bungalow in Titchfield, Hampshire. We are just two minutes walk from the church and shops. Robert calls in every day and - since my illness earlier in the year so does a home-help. We have all we could possibly need. We couldn't be better fixed. All

---

* Kevin and Karen went to Spain exactly 60 years later - to the day - that I left Belfast to go to Congo.

our relatives and Christian friends can see how the Lord has provided for us in our old age. Indeed our God is "no man's debtor".

•••

"There failed not a word of any good thing which the LORD had spoken unto the house of Israel; all came to pass".
Joshua 21: 45.

Postscript

❖

IS THAT THE CORRECT HEADING? SHOULD IT NOT BE
"CHAPTER 19 - UNFINISHED"?

One morning a few months ago Mr. Milliken suddenly felt very
unwell. He struggled to the telephone to phone Robert at his school
and dialled the wrong number. A Christian doctor in membership at
Titchfield Evangelical Church answered. Without knowing who he
was speaking to Mr. Milliken put the receiver down. However the
doctor recognised Mr. Milliken's Ulster accent and realised that
something was wrong. She rushed straight round to the bungalow.
By the time Robert arrived Mr. Milliken had been examined, admit-
tance to hospital arranged, a friend from the church contacted to
come and be with Mrs. Milliken, and the doctor had even packed
Mr. Milliken's suitcase for him. They were just awaiting the ambu-
lance when Rob arrived. The pneumonia was caught in time and
Mr. Milliken has now fully recovered. Letters and cards came from
all over the world assuring them of the prayers of Christian friends.

Now the home-helps call twice a day. While I was visiting the
Milliken's they had a stream of callers - and Mrs. Milliken witnessed

to them all in the direct, uninhibited, unselfconscious manner which for seventy years and more she has employed in Wales and England, Congo and France. It was an inspiring experience to be with them - especially at meal times, which always began with the singing of grace - in French! One of the carers remarked, "We love coming here. They are so different from our other elderly people. They don't live in the past". And it was true - they weren't living on their memories - even of such an eventful past as their's. Mr. and Mrs. Milliken's great concern was the welfare of their church at Titchfield and then of Paulsgrove Baptist and Reston Bible Church and especially of the young people connected with those churches. When there are no callers to counsel or letters to answer they give themselves to the ministry of prayer and intercession.

When asked what piece of advice he would pass on to a young believer setting out along the Christian path today - Mr. Milliken gave me 5! They were "The Lord leads step by step" - "Prepare for guidance through prayer" - "Be ready for anything" -"Hold everything loosely (even our children are lent from the Lord)" - "Never be ashamed of Jesus".

Here, then, are examples of true missionaries - consistently faithful to their calling - continuing to be useful in their Saviour's service. For those who have read this account of the Lord's dealings with Robert and Ivy Milliken prayerfully, basic principles applicable to every Christian believer will have been discerned. What a blessing and encouragement it has been to place their testimony on record. I thank God for granting me this privilege.

CHRIS CLEMENT
Glasgow Bible College, 1995

•••

"Those that be planted in the house of the LORD shall flourish in the courts of our God. They shall still bring forth fruit in old age....."
Psalm 92: 13 & 14.